Pagan Portals

Blacksmith Gods

Myths, Magicians & Folklore

T0159462

Pagan Portals
Blacksmith Gods

Myths, Magicians & Folklore

Pete Jennings

Winchester, UK
Washington, USA

First published by Moon Books, 2014
Moon Books is an imprint of John Hunt Publishing Ltd., Laurel House, Station Approach,
Alresford, Hants, SO24 9JH, UK
office1@jhpbooks.net
www.johnhuntpublishing.com
www.moon-books.net

For distributor details and how to order please visit the 'Ordering' section on our website.

Text copyright: Pete Jennings 2013

ISBN: 978 1 78279 627 5

A CIP catalogue record for this book is available from the British Library.

Design and cover: Stuart Davies
www.stuartdaviesart.com

Printed and bound by CPI Group (UK) Ltd, Croydon, CR0 4YY

We operate a distinctive and ethical publishing philosophy in all
areas of our business, from our global network of authors to
production and worldwide distribution.

CONTENTS

Introduction

Under a spreading chestnut-tree
The village smithy stands;
The smith, a mighty man is he,
With large and sinewy hands;
And the muscles of his brawny arms
Are strong as iron bands.
Henry Wadsworth Longfellow, *The Village Smithy*[1]

That opening verse of a well-known poem gives us a vivid image of a powerfully built artisan. It is a traditional and time-weathered description, which could easily be applied to such craftsmen over a span of thousands of years. Yet within it there are many questions to be asked: is he purely a worker in black metals, making him a blacksmith, or is he a redsmith working in the softer copper or bronze? There are even white smiths, those mainly itinerant tinkers using pewter or tin. Does he wear the split apron of the farrier, a specialist in shoeing horses? Does he work with more precious metals such as gold and silver, intricately setting precious jewels into them, or applying an enamel – a goldsmith or silversmith perhaps? Is he in fact completely physically flawless, or do his unmentioned legs have some deformity?

There is the possibility that he (or today she) will be all of those things, combining skills to provide whatever is required within the community in which he is placed. Nowadays we are used to tradesmen becoming very specialised within a particular niche, but that has not always been the case, and I would hazard a guess that a smith in a small village a couple of centuries ago would have been poorly considered if he could not shoe the horse as well as make a chain for it to haul with. Of course, even then there would have been an elite of better trained, more experienced workers drawn to produce finer quality goods for the gentry. I doubt that the metalworker who created the complex beauty of the 7th century Anglo Saxon Sutton Hoo heavily ornate gold belt buckle (more than 412 grams in weight) would have had his talents wasted by turning out lots of simple horseshoes.

Yet even at the basest level of the smith's craft, a sense of awe, magic and mystery attaches itself. Little wonder, when those early workers of the Bronze Age and Iron Age obtained metal from rocks and turned it into tools and weapons. It was a world away from their stone implement ancestors. We hear about the magical "drawing the sword from the stone" in Arthurian legend, yet that is what those early metalworkers actually achieved. No wonder they kept their trade secrets, making sure that they maintained a local monopoly on such goods. Of course, keeping their secrets from the general population (and working apart from them to prevent the spread of fire) would be bound to lead to an idea or suspicion that they were working some sort of magic; that is actions that could not be explained by other ordinary people. In some places even iron or other metals were imbued with an air of magic, good or bad, and consequently would not be used in ritual situations. Sir James Frazer lists many of these taboos from Africa, Estonia and Poland, Native Americans to ancient Greece, Crete and Rome.[2]

An early trade guild of blacksmiths in London was mentioned in 1299. the Fraternity of St. Loie,[3] which eventually developed into the Blacksmiths Company (1421) and thence the Worshipful Company of Blacksmiths, who received their charter in the reign of Queen Elizabeth 1 in 1571. Originally the various trade guilds were religious in nature, but acted as a friendly society to assist members in poor circumstances and as a body to control and regulate the quality of work including inspecting pieces made by apprentices who wished to become blacksmiths in their own right. Nowadays the company encourages and funds training and quality of work with prizes and bursaries. Its patron saint is

St. Clement (see Chapter 8) and its motto is *"By Hammer and Hand, all Arts do Stand,"* which is very appropriate.[4]

In some cases blacksmiths may actually be working magic, in the sense of doing something unknown to the general understanding of people. I am particularly thinking of farriers: the art of horse magic still has not been completely swept away by mechanisation in my native East Anglia or, I understand, in its other stronghold of Scotland. The ability of a person to control horses to stand still or to move forwards or backwards without any verbal or physical commands is a handy one when trying to nail metal shoes to their hooves. Whilst some of the more inquisitive may have found out about the efficacy of certain secret unguents applied to a toad's bone or other receptacle in the pocket, to most it would remain a wondrous magical ability. The power of the "horseman's grip and word" transmitted orally from one generation to the next in the secretive horsemen's guilds is still little understood or published, yet is respected by many older people who still remember the use of heavy horses and the men who controlled them.

Blacksmithing is woven into our very English language; think of the popular sayings:

"You have to strike while the iron is hot": the meaning is to seize an opportunity before it vanishes. Richard Edwards used the phrase in a play acted before the Queen in 1564[5] called *Damon and Pithias* and it refers to a blacksmith having to work metal whilst it is still retaining heat from the forge.

Having *"too many irons in the fire"* is generally considered a bad thing. A blacksmith would be very busy in that case, and may miss withdrawing an object from the fire at the right moment.

Going at it *"hammer and tongs"* indicates a blacksmith putting a lot of effort into a task.

Something having *"a nice ring to it"* suggests something sounding attractive or good. If a cracked metal or glass vessel is struck it has a dull tone instead of making a clear ringing sound, so no doubt the process would be an easy way to check the quality of a smith's work.

They all derive from the blacksmith's art.

Think too of the wonder of a pattern welded sword or other weapon: as an Anglo Saxon re-enactor I can tell you that the modern public are still fascinated to learn why the best high status swords may have an intricate pattern within the middle of the blade. In some cases it is visible all the time, but in others one has to breathe on the blade to reveal its sinuous serpent-like curves. The process that causes this is lengthy and complicated, and inevitably raises the potential value of the sword. Strips of metal are twisted together and hammered out. The process is repeated many times. The end result is a central core to the sword that is not only visually attractive, but more flexible. A harder metal which is easier to sharpen is then welded around this core to make the cutting edge. Any small mistake in this process will result in many hours of work wasted and the rejection of the finished article. Even with our modern tools and temperature gauges this is a process that only a few of the best sword smiths use, and they command a much higher price for them than the more usual one-piece combined sword blade and tang. Little wonder then that their ancestors would have kept the process secret and encouraged a sense of mystique about their master craftsmanship. To produce a blade that reveals a dragon or serpent when breathed upon still feels magical even when you know the process.

Because of the heavy continuous physical labour employed, the stereotypical blacksmith is very strong, especially in the arms, and in the hot conditions of the forge may work stripped to the waist. That sounds like a desirable image to set ladies' hearts a-flutter in the days before action hero film stars! Such men may well be popular with males too though: an admiration of their skill and physical strength combined with respect for their craftsmanship and semi-independent lifestyle. In many communities, the village forge was a focus for men to gather and talk around the warming fire, so long as they did not get in the way. Even today, a working blacksmith is a character that people like to watch.

Before industrialisation, a community would value having a local blacksmith as a respected inhabitant, and would not want to lose him. He would often be the go-to man for practical problem solving. His family may have occupied the same forge for centuries, using the same inherited tools, anvil and forge and bellows; my late father-in-law, Ron Smith, worked a forge at the small hamlet of Gainsford End, near Castle Hedingham, Essex (now sadly demolished). It is believed to have been worked by his same Smith family for 400 years, only stopping when he failed to have a son or brother willing to carry it on. He eventually gave up when he was affected by severe arthritis, something I have found to be a common complaint in retired smiths. Maybe that contributes to the image of the lame god smith we shall explore.

Ron Smith had the classic surname for his occupation, and it is the most common English surname. Similarly, foreign words for smith have also become common surnames in their respective countries e.g. the Slavic Kovač and Italian Ferrari (yes, the car manufacturer), the French Lefèvre, the Spanish Herrera and Fieraru and the Portuguese Ferreira to name but a few. As we shall see, the figure of a smith as god or demi-god is just as widespread.

I use the designation demi-god deliberately: as you will find, many are not accepted into the ranks of the main gods of their respective mythologies, either because of physical impairment such as the "lame-god" archetype, or because they only have one divine parent. There is a well-known Pagan saying, "As above, so below," or the microcosm reflecting the macrocosm in more modern technical parlance. The liminal status of the smith demi-god, admired but not quite a member of the gods, is reflected by the human smiths of many times and cultures: revered and valued for their technical and sometimes magical prowess, but not accepted as an ordinary member of the communities they serve, and sometimes made to live apart.

The lame god idea is one that has been acknowledged but not investigated to any great degree it seems. I believe that it is something very different to the Jungian "wounded healer" archetype,[6] in as much as the disability of the blacksmith does not aid or inform his work in the same way that a healer uses their own experience of illness or injury to enhance their abilities. I have already said that some smiths suffer in their health as result of their work, e.g. arthritis or burns, but some gods or demi-gods seem to become smiths because of an existing disability or imperfection. E.g. The Greek Hephaestus, rejected by the gods for his ugliness and who then breaks his legs in his fall from Mount Olympus after being cast down from it.

There are other types of god who are disabled in some way but are not blacksmiths. Consider the Norse Tyr (Anglo Saxon Tiw). He loses a hand to the supernaturally fierce and huge Fenris wolf in an act of courage to save the other gods. Whilst once the leader of the gods, he is supplanted by Odin (Anglo Saxon Woden). Yet he is not a smith god. Conversely the Celtic Lugh of the Silver Hand (a replacement for a lost one) is able to maintain his role as leader.

From those same Germanic pantheons we have the thunder and fertility god Thor (Anglo Saxon Thunor) with his mighty war hammer Mjollnir. Despite having a hammer, he is not the smith god either – that role is played by Völundr (Anglo Saxon Wayland Smith). Some smith gods within other countries and cultures do have attributes of fire and thunder or even war, but not in every case. That is why I feel it is misleading to assign one god as the equivalent of another. For example, Wayland seems to be a very different character, with different stories to Völundr, and no connection to war other than making the weapons and armour.

It has not been possible to find a blacksmith god in every country or culture: that could have been for a number of reasons. They may have shared a god with a neighbouring culture. They may have had all Pagan gods suppressed by incoming religions who destroyed all trace of them, particularly if they had few written, sculptural or pictorial records. There have been some cultures in which metalworking was not seen as an important, or not even a local activity worthy of having its own deity. In some cases a god usually associated with other activities or elements e.g. crafts, war, fire etc. may have had smithing added onto their portfolio without the connection surviving in modern records. However, of those cultures that do credit blacksmiths with being sacred, mythological or worthy of being the heroes of stories and customs, I hope you enjoy their stories.

Chapter 1

Classic Sources: Greece and Rome

Greece

Hephaestus

Classic Greek mythology provides us with an archetypal smith god: Hephaestus was the son of the goddess Hera, who had conceived him alone out of spite for Zeus going off with another goddess to have a baby. Apparently he was born ugly and was rejected by the other gods, so was thrown from Mount Olympus (either by Hera or Zeus, depending on which version you read) and smashed his leg landing on the island of Lemnos, causing lameness. (The island became the centre of his cult.) To support himself on earth he learnt the secrets of being a smith and eventually created a cursed throne to trap his mother, then returned to Olympus.

Hephaestus is credited with creating many wonderful things. Homer wrote a detailed description of armour and a shield he made at the request of Thetis for her son Achilles[7] at the siege of Troy. Hephaestus himself was said to have fought at Troy using fire against the river god Skamandros.

He is also credited with creating palaces for the deities of Olympus, so works in more than metal. To top that he was commanded by Zeus to create the woman Pandora as a wife for the Titan Epimetheus, the brother of Prometheus who had angered Zeus. It was a spiteful gift, as she brought a box (or jar) from which she released all the ills of mankind on the world. There are also tales of creatures like robots invented to help him with his work in the volcano that fires his underground forge. He also gave a silver bow and golden arrows to the four-day-old Apollo (son of Leto) to kill a foul smelling snake monster called the Python of Delphi. Hera set it on a mission to chase Leto, who was bearing a child by her husband Zeus.

Hephaestus is credited as the Greek god of fire, smithing, sculpture and stone masons. He is usually pictured as holding a hammer and tongs. Curiously he rides a donkey rather than a horse or chariot. He was married to the beautiful but unfaithful Aphrodite. In the Iliad[8] he speaks to another wife, Kharis, about what he has done:

She [Thetis] saved me when I suffered much at the time of my great fall through the will of my own brazen-faced mother [Hera], who wanted to hide me for being lame. Then my soul would have taken much suffering had not Eurynome and Thetis caught me and held me, Eurynome, daughter of Okeanos, whose stream bends back in a circle. With them I worked nine years as a smith, and wrought many intricate things; pins that bend back, curved clasps, cups, necklaces, working there in the hollow of the cave, and the stream of Okeanos around us went on forever with its foam and its murmur. No other among the gods or among mortal men knew about us except Eurynome and Thetis. They knew since they saved me.

In another case of infidelity closer to home Hephaestus created a net of golden chains which he dropped on his wife Aphrodite as she made love with Ares, the god of war. He tried to shame them by calling the gods to witness them, but some refused and others sympathised with Ares saying it was worth being trapped in chains to make love with the beautiful Aphrodite. Yet Hephaestus wasn't above being unfaithful himself, and tried unsuccessfully to rape the virginal Athena. His semen fell to Earth instead and resulted in the Earth producing Erikhthonios, who was brought up as a foster child by Athena.

Hephaestus certainly was no goody goody god: he also created a necklace that cursed Harmonia and her descendants to continuing tragedy. However, he became valued by the gods, creating a staff for Agamemnon, a chariot for Helios, a breast-plate for Aegis, Hermes' winged sandals and archery gear for Eros and Artemis, as well as Apollo.

Kabeiroi

One source also lists Kabeiroi / Cabeiroi as an order of Greek blacksmith gods connected to a Samothrace and Lemnos mystery cult, possibly children of Hephaestus[9] who were deliberately never named individually. Some think they are a pre-Hellenic (possibly Phrygian or Hittite) group of divinities who survived the invasion of the Aegean Islands by the Greeks.

The Cyclops

The Cyclops pre-date Hephaestus within the Greek mythology as smiths and creators, since they were credited with originally building Olympus for the gods. They do not seem to be classed as gods or demi-gods themselves, and are of an enormous size, with one eye. There is a theory that this relates to the practice of some blacksmiths wearing an eye patch over one eye to prevent blinding by sparks in both eyes at once.

Odysseus and his sailors met with one on an island with a large goat pen. After they had eaten some goats, it turned out they were owned by a Cyclops called Polythemus, who thought eating them in turn would be a good recompense for his lost herd!

Please be aware that, as in most mythologies, there are generally several alternative versions and names etc. This not only applies within the Greek mythology I have quoted above, but becomes even more confusing when it is recast later by the Romans who alter names and some details, but use very similar stories.

Dactyls

Although the Cyclops were sometimes said to have been the first to forge metal, iron at least was supposed to be the discovery of the Dactyls of Phrygia who had watched Mount Ida erupt. They seem to also have a reputation as powerful magicians, and their names were invoked for protection.

Rome

Vulcan

Vulcan, the Roman equivalent of the Greek Hephaestus, is unusual in that he is seen as a god of both beneficial and destructive fire, and that latter characteristic is linked to his dominion over volcanoes. The term volcano seems to have derived from a volcanic island of that name in the Mediterranean, near Sicily. The inhabitants credited the fumes and debris of the active volcano as evidence of Vulcan using it as a forge. There he was reputed to make, amongst other things, weapons for the war god Mars and thunderbolts for the supreme god Jupiter (or Jove).

There is a curious tale of how he first possessed fire: as a youngster he played with the dolphins in the sea, but became fascinated by a fisherman's fire. From it he took a burning ember and enclosed it in the shell of a clam.

Taking the glowing ember back to his boyhood den, he experimented with it. First he watched it, and then he blew on it and found it glowed hotter. Making bellows he found that some rocks could melt under extreme heat to produce metals. With a hammer that became his symbol, he beat the metal into all sorts of tools, weapons and jewellery. Undoubtedly he created horseshoes too, because a mosaic (picturing the Battle of Issus) from Pompeii shows a horse that has been shod in that era.

Vulcan also became a part of the myth of Orion. This myth seems at times to include elements of both the convoluted and contradictory Roman and Greek mythologies, but I will try to give a simple version here.

Orion was supposedly a gift from the gods (with a multitude of competing mythical parents) to a favoured peasant, and was able to walk on water (not a unique accomplishment if one consults the Christian Bible) and had enormous strength. With his strength he became a skilled blacksmith, and attempted to seize Princess Merope as a lover. Her father did not approve, even when his potential son-in-law rid the land of vicious wild beasts (giving him his main attribute as a great hunter). He got him drunk and blinded him.

Orion followed the sound of the Cyclops' hammer to Lemnos (presumably one working for Vulcan). Vulcan gave him a man called Kedalion to be his guide to the East, where the Greek sun god Apollo Helios (or Roman Sol) healed his sight. Orion joined Diana (Roman Artemis) in hunting, but her brother Apollo worried for her chastity and, when sending a scorpion to him failed, tricked her into shooting him as he waded up to his neck through the sea. Distraught, she placed him in the sky as a constellation at the opposite side of the sky to Scorpius.

I will accept that Vulcan / Hephaestus only seems to play a minor part in this tale of Orion. However, it does seem to confirm a Cyclops working for him on his island. One could also speculate that in helping Orion he would also be annoying the king, and any god that particularly supported him. There are always consequences and in the hopelessly complex labyrinth that is Greco-Roman mythology one never knows where one story intrudes or gives rise to another.

Chapter 2

Africa, Asia & Beyond

Africa

Some tribes in West Africa are reported as regarding the local blacksmith as a religious priest, from a superior descent than their fellow tribesmen. Additionally, some tribes have a specific blacksmith god: the Ga tribe acknowledge Gua, and the Yoruba tribe (also from West Africa) have Ogun. Interestingly, Ogun is also the name for a smith god from Hawaii. In Namibia there is a creator god, Tsunigoab Khoi, who limps. It is unusual for a creator god to be a lame god, but he is also important for smiths.

Several tribes (such as the Baralongs from South Africa) regard the process of smelting and forging as sacred, and keep it as a reserved occupation for an elite group of tribesmen. It is reported that the Tibbous of Central Africa and people in Abyssinia and the Congo regard iron workers with respect, deference and give them the reputation of magicians.

In the Fan tribe the chief is also the medicine man and smith, as none but chiefs are allowed to deal with such sacred activities.[10]

However, this does not always lead to esteem: Monbiot[11] tells of an excursion to the El Barta Plains of Kenya. He interviewed Ntalon, a tall shaven-headed woman in red from the blacksmith clan of her Samburu tribe. She said that they were: "Polluted by malevolent powers. They could cause a wound inflicted with iron to fester, or bring about the death of a child circumcised with an iron razor. Anyone of another clan who stepped over an Nkunono's forge would break his legs. Their isolation and pollution were reinforced by their constraint to commit what the Samburu regard as incest, by marrying only among themselves. She and her people had to remain apart from the other

Samburu."

Monbiot goes on to theorise why the situation should exist, drawing upon the evidence that in the Lake Victoria area the anvil was the symbol of sacred kingship. He conjectured that the smiths of that area had used their powerful positions to take political control as tyrants over the people. The smith god Ogun was amongst the most important of the Orisha deities.

The god of war, of the hunt, and of ironworking, Ogun serves as the patron deity of blacksmiths, warriors, and all who use metal in their occupations. He also presides over deals and contracts; in fact, in Yoruba courts, devotees of the faith swear to tell the truth by kissing a machete sacred to Ogun. The Yoruba consider Ogun fearsome and terrible in his revenge; they believe that if one breaks a pact made in his name, swift retribution will follow.

Furthermore, in countries as diverse as Tanzania, Ethiopia and Morocco, the *boudas* (a term for a sorcerer / blacksmith) can turn into a were-hyena!

A Kamba tribal folktale from Kenya was collected by Kieti and Coughlin.[12] It tells of a blacksmith who goes away from home to work. His wife Kikyele stays behind with her three children. An ogre disguised as a servant eats each child, one at a time, and then even her new-born babe. Kikyele is suspicious of how they are disappearing, and eventually finds out. However, she has problems in finding her husband, so she spread sorghum to dry and, after two unsuccessful attempts with other birds, she lures a pigeon to eat, which she trains to repeat a message to her husband. It flies off to find him, and eventually homes in on the sound of hammer on metal. It sings to him:

You, busy blacksmith, saa-ngalala. What are you making? Saa-ngalala. Your wife gave birth, saa-ngalala, and invited an ogre, saa-ngalala, who knows how to cook and serve, saa-ngalala.

The husband rushes home and finds all his cattle and children gone, eaten by the ogre. He slashes its neck with a machete, and it tells him to cut its little finger and toe, which he does. All the children and animals spurt out. The ogre is killed and the couple are left cuddling their children and putting the animals back in the pen.

Arabia

In the south of the country the god Qasynan holds sway over smithing. When the Arabs of the Sahara Desert were in battle they would spare the life of a man who dismounted from his horse, knelt and mimed the actions of working bellows with the corners of his cloak. In a culture obsessed with horses one can understand the preservation of a man showing that he is a farrier.

Egypt

One ancient Egyptian god of blacksmithing does not seem to have been a prominent one within their complex mythology. His name is Keserty, detailed on an Egyptian stela, and is equated with a similar Canaanite blacksmith god called Kōshar. They have gazelle heads on their headdresses instead of the more usual snake.[13] There was also Knutim (Kneph, Knemu) who makes humans on a potter's wheel as well as being a metalcraft god. He is joined by Ptah who has a multitude of tasks: metalwork, masonry, architecture and the sunrise.

Morocco

Morocco has an unusual traditional form of pygmy smith. They wear an outer garment called a *haik*, which has a single eye decorating the back, maybe as a symbol of the Cyclops. In any case, the Haratin tribesmen of the Drah valley think it wrong to even mention their name, which they respect as magicians and healers. One of their specialities is to make miniature books used as amulets.[14]

Syria

Syria has the blacksmith god Kotar, also spelt Kautar and Kusar. The name Kotar is common with that of the ancient Canaanite god.

Hittites

Within their ancient culture, the Hittites had the sacred Hasameli for smiths.

Asia

Apparently some magicians in Hindustan sprinkle water from a blacksmith's forge as part of their rites for demonic possession. They say that it is extra effective since hot iron has been repeatedly quenched in it.

Some blacksmith groups in Central Asia have tried to keep their craft secret, and perform a festival of wild dancing with clashing weapons, cymbals and tambourines to intimidate others with their magic.

Tvastar or Vishvakarma is the Hindu blacksmith of the devas, and there is reference to him in the very ancient Rigveda text. It is possible that the name Tattar, applied to goldsmiths in South India, may derive from the god's name Tvastar.

Guam

Guam is an island in the Micronesian Mariana Islands of the Pacific Ocean. It has a rather wonderful folktale about a god called Chaife.[15] He is the god of their volcanic underworld *Sasalâguan* (Hell), commands all the elements and is a creator smith.

They believed… that the souls of those who died a natural death descended to an underworld paradise where there were "bananas, coconuts, sugar cane and other fruits of the earth". On the other hand, the souls of those who died a violent death went to a sort of hell

*called Sasalåguan, the dwelling place of Chayfi, a demon, who
cooked them in a cauldron which he stirred continually.*[16]

Once, as Chaife was cooking some souls, the fire burned very
fiercely and blew up, releasing ash, cinders and rocks. One of
his tortured souls was blown clear also, and fell into the sea
near Humåtak (Umatac). The soul was so hot it turned to rock
as it plunged into the waves. The waves gradually wore it
away into the shape of the first Chamarro man. He was happy
to have escaped and to land in the beautiful land of Guam,
but eventually became a bit lonely. So, remembering how he
had been created, he took some clay and molded it into other
people, the "children of the earth" which he brought to life by
laying them out in the sun.

Chaife was furious when he eventually found out one of
his souls had escaped, but thought he had found it when he
saw a child on the shore. In his fury he created a wave to
drown the child, but it simply turned into a fish and swam
away. So he drew upon fire to boil away the water of the bay,
but the fish just turned into a lizard. The lizard scuttled for
cover into the jungle, so Chaife set fire to the jungle, but like
a phoenix, out of the ashes came a bird that flew up into the
clear blue sky. "I have you now," thought Chaife, as he called
upon the element of wind in a mighty hurricane. The bird
crashed into a cliff, but as it slid down it changed back to the
child on the shore again.

In a clear voice it sang out: "Chaife, you may command
fire, waves and wind, but my soul comes from the sun, so you
cannot destroy me."

"But that cannot be!" was the angry reply. "I created you
as my slave soul in Sasalåguan."

"Ha!" laughed the child, "that's what you think, but the
soul that escaped is at Foula Bay, making many more sun
souls like me that you cannot harm."

Of course, Chaife sped there trying to find him, but by then he had turned back to a rock, and the god realized that he had been outwitted, and slunk back to his hell.

China

Ch'I-You is the Chinese god of smiths, war, weapons and surprisingly dancers.

Japan

Ama-Tsu-Mara is the Japanese Shinto god of smiths. He only has one eye, and made a mirror to reflect the sun and so bring Amaterasu out of hiding. There is also another deity called Tama-No-Ya who particularly looks after jewellers.

Fine swordsmiths are still revered in Japan, but none more so than the legendary Masamune. His best sword could cut everything bad whilst preserving the innocent and pure. Yet another master blacksmith has a wonderful tale told about him:

Back in the 10th century a great blacksmith called Munetschika created the best swords, and each one was even better than the last he had forged. The Emperor Jtschijo was on the throne, but when he died his successor Sanjo upset the Koreans who Japan had conquered, and started a war. Divinations agreed that a new sword was needed in their defeat, and of course Munetschika was commanded to create it. To do that he needed an even mightier forge, and was sent a great warrior called Taschibana to help him create it. But he was concerned that he had no other worthy assistants for the greatest task he had ever undertaken.

The goddess Inari sent a white fox who told him everything would be alright, and helped him as well as any apprentice could have done. The sword was produced, and when he proudly put his seal on the work found that next to it another appeared – the image of the white fox. The sword was presented to the Emperor in Kyoto, and gifted to his general, of the Taira family. At the crucial battle against Korea the sword was drawn and victory gained, and the Sword of the Fox has remained an important part of the Imperial Treasury since then.

Mesopotamia, Babylon and Akkadian

These cultures share Ninegal. The name means "strong armed lord", which is certainly apt, but the character must not be confused with a goddess of the same name who is an aspect of the Sumerian goddess Inanna.

Persia (Now Iran)

I found this unique blacksmith story from Persia.[17] It was based upon the *Shah Nemeh* (Book of Kings) which contains the legendary history of Persia, including the story of Gavah the Blacksmith:

To myth again must we go for our earliest blacksmith rebel, Zohak, the son of a usurping King of Persia. Early in his manhood he came under the spell of Eblis, the Evil One, who persuaded him to murder his father, and so succeed to the throne. This Zohak did, and during his reign Eblis devised daily new tyrannies, which the king imposed on the people. Now, Eblis was the inventor of the art of cookery and constantly delighted the King's palate with new dishes. One day he excelled himself, with no less a dish than a boiled egg. So delighted was Zohak that he promised Eblis any boon he might ask. The Evil One replied with a request to be allowed to kiss the bare shoulders of the King; and in response to the caress of the lips of the fiend two vipers grew up from the monarch's shoulders. The creatures twined and hissed, demanding food. Eblis assured the King that nothing would satisfy the monsters save the brains of men, and advised him to draw up a census of his subjects. This the King did, and as no national volunteers were forthcoming, conscription was immediately introduced. Each day saw the brain pans of two citizens of Iran spilt of their precious content to satisfy the hell-gotten monsters that had sprang from the corrupt carcass of royalty.

So things went on, until one day the lots were drawn against the two sons of Gavah, the blacksmith. But rather than submit tamely the blacksmith prepared to meet tyranny with insurrection; and Gavah's forge became the Altar of Liberty. A great army gathered, and was armed by Gavah and his sons. All was ready to march against the tyrant, when Gavah thought that a flag was necessary. So he nailed his leathern apron to a pike, and held it aloft. But at this moment another army appeared. It was Feridum, the rightful king, who joined his forces with those of Govah, and together they overthrew Zohak. The vanquished tyrant escaped to the mountains, where he took refuge in a cave, only to be eaten alive by the vipers that still writhed and hissed about his head.

Whoever does not believe this story is referred to the flag of Persia, which to the present day takes the form of a blacksmith's leathern apron, adorned with the jewels of Feridun.

Chapter 3

English and Germanic Sources

I have combined English and Germanic sources since the first often derives from the latter, in that the Anglo Saxons were of a Germanic origin. Those whom they conquered, have their own chapters to follow. I have placed Sigmund's story with the Scandinavian material, since although it is located in Germany, it was adopted and spread by the Scandinavians.

The blacksmith god does not have the monopoly of healing horses, an ancillary part of the blacksmith's art before the days of veterinary surgeons. The *Merseberg Charms*, written in High German into a 10th century liturgical book, preserves two Pagan spells, probably from the 9th century. The *Second Merseberg Charm*[18] concerns healing a lame horse:

Phol and Wodan were riding to the woods,
and the foot of Balder's foal was sprained
So Sinthgunt, Sunna's sister, conjured it.
and Frija, Volla's sister, conjured it.
and Wodan conjured it, as well he could:
Like bone-sprain, so blood-sprain,
so joint-sprain:
Bone to bone, blood to blood,
joints to joints, so may they be glued.

There is a similarly structured Norwegian Christian charm, with Jesus as the rider and healer. Who Phol is has been the subject of much inconclusive academic debate. Personally I go with Frey, since an alternative of Balder does not make much sense when his usual name is used in the next line. One other possibility may be Thor, as another phallic god. There are some Anglo Saxon verse charms[19] that have survived also, but they seem to have been heavily Christianised, or been Christian in origin.

Other supernatural beings performing skilful smith work include the dwarves in Norse mythology, (and maybe by association related Anglo Saxon myths), but we will get to them when we look at Scandinavia.

In Germany, forges are sometimes known as Weiland's Houses, after probably the best known smith demi-god, Wayland Smith (also known as Weyland, Weland and Weiland Smith). The term "wei" or "weihs" is thought by some to mean sacred, so for example Wayland Wood near Watton, Norfolk, may refer to a woodland originally associated with a sacred site, maybe important for Pagan rituals or pilgrimage. The much diminished woodland has legendary status as a place named in the story of Edmund, king and saint, where his decapitated head is found by followers to be guarded by a wolf. It is also the location for the loss of the Babes in the Wood from nearby Griston Hall, where their wicked uncle had ordered their death.

In their dictionary, The Brothers Grimm stated that the Gothic word "weihs" meant "sacred", but also to "curve or bend". They also connected the term with the Ingvaeonic word "wikkōn", which is believed to connect into the English term Wicca, a form of witchcraft associated both with "bending" and "wise".[20]

It used to be the custom in South Germany and the Austrian Tyrol for a blacksmith to hit three blows on the anvil with his hammer every Saturday night when he finished work. It was said that somehow this chained the Devil up for the coming week. Hitting the anvil every so often between beating out a horseshoe is said to be done for the same reason. Blacksmiths are supposed to be quite good at recognising the Devil in disguise, as the folk tale of Gossensass in Tyrol shows:

The smith was asked to shoe two pitch black horses by a mysterious handsome gentleman. When the work was done, he was asked the price. "No money," came the surprising reply, "just never enter here again." The gentleman agreed to keep the promise, and hasn't been seen there since.

Rudyard Kipling tells a tale of Weland Smith in *Puck of Pook's Hill*, and consequently he has been discovered by many young readers. Puck declares:

Weland gave the Sword, The Sword gave the Treasure, and the Treasure gave the Law. It's as natural as an oak growing.[21]

Walter Scott names a character after him in *Kenilworth*[22] but it is not the demi-god, just a character named after him. A Neolithic long barrow and chambered stone tomb on the Ridgeway near the Uffington White Horse, Oxfordshire (originally Berkshire before boundary changes), is named Wayland Smithy. Apparently it originated as a timber-lined oval barrow in around 3700 BCE, which was changed to a stone chambered long barrow in about 3400 BCE, three hundred years later. The legend says that if a horse is left there overnight with sixpence, it will be re-shod in the morning so long as no one tries to spy on what happens.

The knowledge of a site known as Wayland Smithy (also known as Wayland's Stocc) seems to have been quite widespread, and Pollington[23] notes that it is mentioned in a West Saxon charter of 855 CE, and that the character is also referred to in Somerset, England, as well as in Belgium, Germany, Denmark and Norway.

The opening verse of the Old English Anglo Saxon poem *Deor*[24] says this about him:

Weland himself, by means of worms
experienced agony,
the strong-minded noble
endured troubles;
he had for his companions

sorrow and longing,
winter-bitter wrack,
he often found misery
after Niðhad
put fetters on him,
supple sinew-bonds
on the better man.
That was overcome,
so may this be.

Deor is believed to be of an 8th century Anglian source by Alexander[25] and others. Wayland Smith is also featured in the awesome Anglo Saxon tale of *Beowulf* as creator of the mail shirt worn by Beowulf[26] and in the poem *Waldere*[27], in which the eponymous hero wields the sword Miming made by Wayland. In the incomplete opening lines:

... bravely urged him
Surely Welund's work does not betray
Any man who can hold Mimming hard

Within the Anglo Saxon charm (British Library Manuscript Harley 585, from circa 1000 CE) to ease a sudden stitch, along with making a herbal concoction, there are instructions to make a magical knife with various verses said during its production, including the following:

The smith sat, hammered out a little knife,
(an article of) iron, very wondrously,
Out, little spear, if (any) here be within!
Six smiths sat, made killing spears,
Out, little spear, not in, spear![28]

It is possible that the charm links in to the idea of some illnesses and conditions being caused by "elf shot" i.e. supernatural means.

He is even mentioned by Alfred the Great in a commentary within his English translation of the 6th century Roman philosopher Boëthius.[29]

King Alfred the Great is actually the focus of one story about blacksmiths, told originally by Sebillot.[30] He is reported to have gathered seven of his main craftsmen and said he would make one of them the chief craftsman, so long as he was able to manage without the work of the others. They were all invited to attend a banquet with a sample of their work and the tools that made it. There was, of course, much excitement, because each privately thought that they were indispensable.

The baker had the shovel he used with the oven, and on it a fine loaf of bread. After all, we all have to eat. The blacksmith proudly flourished his hammer and a horseshoe; the shoemaker had his awl and a beautiful pair of shoes, the carpenter a finished plank of wood and his saw. Everyone smiled to see the butcher brandish his cleaver over a juicy cut of meat. Less exciting was the mason with a trowel and finished corner stone, but they had to agree that buildings were important. However, it was the tailor who was chosen to be the chief with his scissors and newly made clothes. Who could do without them? The blacksmith was, to say the least, not happy with their decision. Without a word he skulked off, closed down his smithy and said he would not work there any more for such ungrateful fellow craftsmen.

It wasn't long before King Alfred's horse lost a shoe, but of course none of the other craftsmen could help him. The tailor soldiered on for as long as he could, but they all had to admit that they would have to try to do the blacksmith's work. What a disaster! The tailor burnt his fingers, the baker got kicked by the horse and the butcher dropped a heavy bar of metal on his toe. None of them could do the job, and they all started blaming each other for the bad decision. The argument became a fight and in the disturbance the old anvil crashed over with a loud bang!

At this point Saint Clement appeared, leading the blacksmith back. King Alfred greeted them warmly, and admitted that it had all been a mistake, and that he would now proclaim the blacksmith as chief craftsman. To show that there were no hard feelings, the blacksmith made them each a present: a baking tin for the baker, for the shoemaker a hammer, the carpenter got some nails, the mason a chisel, and there was even some new needles for the tailor. Finally he produced a shiny crown for King Alfred, who was so pleased that he commanded each to sing a song. The last to sing was the blacksmith, who sang a song so sweetly called *The Blacksmith* that it is still popular today.

The Story of Wayland Smith

I have so far alluded several times to Wayland Smith, but now let me try to tell his story. Inevitably it draws upon individual elements of several contradictory versions of the tale. In Britain his father is credited as being the god Wade, but that is contradicted in Old Norse sources. Forgive the author if the tale omits some favourite feature of a version with which you are familiar, but there is no way they could all be satisfactorily be combined together and simultaneously make sense. The legend has taken a life of its own, although the earliest likely source is *The Lay of Völundr*[31] from the 13th century Icelandic *Poetic Edda*. It was probably transmitted orally from one generation to the next for centuries before it was committed to writing.

Wayland Smith was the greatest smith of his age. He could make anything in metal, from the finest golden jewellery to the sharpest sword. His reputation spread far and wide and he was never short of people wanting him to make them the finest of objects in gold, silver or iron. Inevitably his reputation reached the ears of King Nidud, an evil tyrant who ruled that land. He sent for Wayland to appear before him. "I hear that you make the finest weapons in the world," said Nidud, eyeing him suspiciously. "Is that true?" Being such a liar himself he never trusted anyone else.

"Well your Majesty," said Wayland modestly, "some kind people have said that."

"Good," replied Nidud, "from now on you can make them for me – I am planning to invade our neighbouring kingdom!"

"I will be pleased to work for you, but I must first finish the goods I have already promised to other people," suggested Wayland.

"How dare you!" shouted Nidud. "I am the king and you will do what I say, at once! Guards, take him away – you know what to do," he added with a grim gesture.

With that Wayland was taken away to a small island in a fast flowing river. They brought his tools and anvil and put them into a derelict, leaking hovel. Most cruelly of all, they bent Wayland over his own anvil and slashed his leg tendons so he could not run or swim away. Leaving him with some fuel and iron, as well as enough food for a week, he was instructed to make lots of good swords. If he did not have them ready when they returned in a week, he would get no more food, and would starve to death. What else could he do but obey? When they were gone he took a dreadful solemn oath on his ring before his gods, that no matter how long, or how hard, he would wreak a horrendous revenge on King Nidud for what he had done, even if he could see no way of achieving it at the moment. Oaths really meant something in those days, and people who intended to keep a good reputation kept to them.

The weary weeks went by, and turned into long months. Wayland slaved away each week to produce the weapons, and a boat came with guards to take them away, leaving fuel, iron and meagre food that had to last him the week, washed down with dirty river water.

Meanwhile, King Nidud sat in his castle, gloating over the great store of fine weapons he was amassing. He had his daughter Badhild for company, and two sons. Otwin, the future heir rode around the kingdom gathering extortionate taxes for his greedy father accompanied by his brother Olwin. One day Eigil, the brother of Wayland, visited while trying to find him. The king entertained him without telling him what he had done. He thought by keeping him at court he may have another way to apply pressure for Wayland to stay working for him. The guards had reported that Wayland's legs were healing and getting stronger. Word was sent to Wayland that his brother Eigil and his son may be in danger if he escaped. Wayland began gathering birds' feathers from the many that landed on the island.

One day when he was bored King Nidud summonsed Eigil before him. "I understand from my courtiers that you are a good archer. I would like to watch you perform with the bow – come!" He led Eigil to a courtyard where to his horror he found his young son with an apple balanced on his head. He performed as the king demanded, splitting the apple in two without harming his son. Noticing that he had two more arrows, the king queried whether he thought he may miss the target?

"No," retorted Eigil, "if I had hit my son the other two were for you!"

"I doubt my guards would have allowed that to happen," taunted the king.

Meanwhile, the two princes having got bored with beating up peasants were looking for some other thing to divert them. Realising that they were near where the fabulous smith was kept, they bullied the boatman to take them to him. Wayland Smith spotted them sailing over the water, and in an instant seized his chance to fulfil his chilling oath. It would take guile and skill, and he had both.

As they strode up the beach he greeted them deferentially, doffing his hat. "Oh your Royal Highnesses," he flattered, "how honoured I am that such noble princes should visit the lowly Wayland at his work." They sneered and looked in disdain at his dirty rags, calloused hands and work-weary face. Then pointing at the sword on Otwin's belt scabbard, he begged a closer look. Warily, Otwin agreed.

"Oh what shoddy workmanship," cried Wayland. "You deserve the finest of weapons to go with your positions, yet the king seems to have palmed you off with second best!"

The brothers were shocked, but not really surprised; they had been taught early in life to think the worst of everyone, including their father. "Come back tomorrow and I will have weapons much more suitable for you," offered Wayland. "I dare not send them via the guards – they may not reach you. Please do not tell anyone, especially the king though, or you will get me into great trouble." The princes agreed to keep the secret and return in a day with the boatman.

When they returned the island the next day, they could not see Wayland. "I bet he is still asleep, the lazy peasant!" said Otwin.

"Or giving the swords a last polish before handing them over – he wouldn't dare to give us anything dirty," suggested the younger brother.

"Huh! You prattle on like an old washerwoman," chided Otwin. "You must learn to be a man of action like me!" With that Otwin strode up to the hovel, kicked open the door and went inside. From behind the door Wayland struck with a very sharp axe he had made, and Otwin's head lay on the floor. Pushing the head and corpse out of the way, Wayland resumed his position behind the door.

"I bet my brother is choosing the best sword for himself," thought Olwin. Taking his brother's example, he too pushed through the door, and he too was soon decapitated. Working quickly, Wayland tossed the heads into a cauldron of boiling water heating on the forge fire. They bubbled and hissed, losing the hair, skin and even the eyeballs. Weyland took them out with a pair of tongs, and as soon as they had cooled, sawed the tops off. He melted metal onto them, and made a stand for each, with beautiful decorations adorning them both. He had produced two goblets from the skulls. Going down to the boatman who had been commanded to wait for the princes, he offered him a great reward if he would complete a couple of tasks for him: deliver the goblets to King Nidud and say that Wayland was afraid to send them via the guards. Whilst he was looking at them, go give a note to Princess Badhild, and another to Eigil. The note to Eigil was to give him some instructions, as well as telling him to give the boatman some gold as a reward. The boatman readily agreed. He had no love for the brutish Nidud, and with gold could escape and make a better life for himself. He did as he was asked.

King Nidud was very impressed with the stylish goblets the boatman brought him, and started boasting how he would show them off at a feast that night, and would make everyone envious. Taking his chance, the boatman slipped the note into Badhild's private chamber, and went to find Eigil, who true to Wayland Smith's word rewarded him when he had read the instructions his brother had sent to him.

The note to the Princess invited her to go to the island secretly: the craftsman had made her some beautiful jewellery, but wanted to make sure it fitted and that it went directly to her. Always keen to adorn herself better than the other ladies of the court, she secretly slipped away. When she reached the island with the boatman, she told him to wait by the shore, and walked to the smithy with eager anticipation of what she may receive, as she had seen the quality of the goblets given to her father. Instead, as she stepped inside she was grabbed and raped by Wayland Smith. As she cried afterwards, Wayland Smith told her why he had done it: to gain revenge on her father who had treated him so cruelly. "The boatman will drop you off on land, and when you see the king you can tell him that last night he drunk from the skulls of his two sons. Their bodies have now washed away by the tide. The only heir that he will have is the bastard son I have left in you, who will eventually usurp and kill his grandfather, meaning that my blood relation will rule in his place!"

"He will catch you, torture you and kill you for this!" yelled Badhild.

"I don't think he will," replied Wayland Smith. With that he put on the wings he had made from birds' feathers and thin strips of metal, and flew up into the sky to Nidud's castle. Of course, everyone came out to see the incredible sight of him hovering in the wind above the walls, including Nidud plus Eigil and his son. "Last night you drunk from the skulls of your sons I killed!" cried Wayland, "and I have made your daughter pregnant as well. That is what you get for your treatment of me."

"Quick Eigil!" barked the King. "If you value the life of your son, shoot him with this arrow." A single arrow was given to Eigil, who aimed carefully before loosing it into the sky. It hit Wayland Smith beneath his outstretched arm, and blood fell in great drops and splashed to the ground as he flew away.

"Well done," said Nidud to Eigil. He will not get far bleeding like that, and will soon die. You may leave with your son as your reward." Without a word Eigil left with his boy, before Nidud could change his mind. It was much later when he met up with his brother, and they both laughed about the skin bag of animal blood that Wayland Smith had concealed beneath his arm.

You will find out some more about Wayland Smith in the chapter 7, in his Norse equivalent Völundr, who is allegedly of Finnish origin, which is significant because the Norse peoples sometimes used Finns as foreign specialist magicians.

Chapter 4

Ireland, Wales and the Isle of Man

Ireland

Human blacksmiths were accorded magical status in Ireland, as elsewhere, and there is a phrase *"briochta ban agus gabann agus druad"* (the spells of women and smiths and druids) that reflects that belief. The status of men such as Nethin (Nectin), the chief blacksmith at Tara in the *Suiduigud Tige Midchuarta*, was also connected to supernatural objects and places in an old law:

> *Three things which confer status on a blacksmith; the cooking spit of Nethin[3], the cooking spit of the Morrígan, the anvil of Dagda.*

There are several competing candidates for the role of blacksmith god in Ireland, maybe reflecting the various Celtic tribes who competed against each other to rule the beautiful place.

Brighid and Ruadan

As one of the best remembered and popular Celtic goddesses, Brighid (also known as Brid, Bride, Brigid) has an enormous number of attributes, including the fire of metalworking and patroness of blacksmiths alongside poetic inspiration, healing, fertility and divination. Her son Ruadan was fathered by Bres, a half Formorii ruler of the magical Tuatha De Danaan tribe. Ruadan was a blacksmith, so he was the ideal person to send as a spy on the smith god Goibniu in the preparation for the second battle of Magh Turedh. Approaching him unseen, Ruadan grabbed a spear he had been making and seized his chance to kill him by plunging it deeply into the god's stomach. Goibniu was not that easy to kill, and simply pulled it out, turned it round and stuck it into Ruadan, who died. The custom of keening (showing physical grief) was said to be started by Brighid as she mourned her son. Brighid was later Christianised as St. Brighid.

Another obscure blacksmith character is Creidhne of the Tuatha De Danaan, but little seems to be known of him.

Goibniu

Goibniu seems to be especially associated with making effective weapons that seldom failed, especially the spears from that last tale of Ruadan. His father Esarg was an axe thrower. Maybe Ruadan was trying to spy on his metalworking methods as much as the military formation and strength of his tribe. Goibniu's name has a talismanic nature, to be called upon in invocations for protection against weapons (and injury by thorns), and is also spelt Gabha, Gaihnann and Gobnenn.

To be healed of his wounds he travelled from his forge, Cerdchae Ghaibhnenn, to the family of Dian Cecht, who guarded the magic waters of the Well of Slaine. Afterwards he was able to return to work making the best of weapons for the Tuatha Dé Dannan tribe, who were victorious over the Fomorians in taking over Ireland.

Goibniu also created the special spear for Lugh that stabbed Balor's eye. Smithing has always been hot, thirsty work, so it is maybe not surprising that Goibniu is also associated with drinking ale and mead. He is said eventually to have died of a plague.

Lugh

Lugh is another member of that troublesome Tuatha Dé Dannan race, and goes on their behalf to see King Nuada of the Silver Hand at Tara. Despite telling them who he is and what his skills are (blacksmith, poet, warrior etc.) they refuse him entry. Eventually he makes the argument that no one else can do all of those things, and they let him in.

Culain

This Irish blacksmith Culain (or Culann) was famous for keeping a ferocious guard dog. He invited King Connor and his court to his home for a feast, showing what high company leading blacksmiths mixed in. When the feast was ready King Connor was asked if everyone was present, and he agreed they were, forgetting that his young friend Setanta was out playing a game of hurling with some of the locals. So Culain left his fearsome guard dog chained outside to protect the house and his noble guests.

When the young Setanta eventually returned, he was attacked by the dog. Having no weapons other than the bat and ball from hurling, he threw the ball hard down its throat. Whilst it struggled, he hit it with the bat, grabbed it and dashed its head on the ground, killing it. With all the noise and commotion the feast quickly broke up as the guests came to the door, expecting an intruder to have been ripped to shreds. Instead the saw the bloodied Setanta, standing over the corpse of the enormous beast. King Connor was upset that he had forgotten his friend and put him into mortal danger, and Culain was upset at the loss of his dog, although he did not blame Setanta for defending himself. Setanta apologised, and offered to take the hound's place, guarding Culain and the valley into Ulster where he lived. The offer was accepted, and since then he was renamed as the hero CuCuhulain, the Hound of Culain.

Creda is also named as a localised, lesser known blacksmith god.

The Isle of Man

The Manx people hold Saint Brighid dear to them. She is the Christianised equivalent of the earlier Pagan goddess Brid or Brigid, a process that happened to some other popular goddesses such as Elen, who became St. Helen. In the Isle of Man, Saint Brighid has many attributes, including patroness of blacksmiths, and they hold a feast day which in the local Gaelic dialect is called Laa'l Breeshey. On the feast day, they welcome her to their homes with a rush bed in the hearth and prayers. The anvil is seen as her symbol.

Wales

King Arthur

The original kingdom of Wales (which went as far north as the Wirral on Merseyside) is the geographic base for many of the Arthurian legends. Enough has been written about their origins and meanings elsewhere to fill a library of books, but I would remind you that the future King Arthur pulls the sword from the stone[32] to prove his worthiness. There are at least two swords connected with King Arthur: Excalibur, which is pulled from the stone, and the Welsh named Caledfwich, which is possibly the one given by the Lady of the Lake and eventually returned to her. Some writers appear to muddle the two together, and no definite maker is suggested for either of them.

There is another sword taken from a stone floating down the river by Sir Galahad when he arrives at Camelot. Whether the sword in the stone story is an allegory for extracting metal from rocks and working with it to produce a weapon is for you to decide. There is a similarity between this action and that of the Germanic Sigmund who pulls a sword called Gram from Barnstokki (a great wooden pillar) that had been placed there by Odin.

Saint Ffraid and Saint Brighid

Saint Ffraid is the partial equivalent of Saint Brighid in Wales, with several churches dedicated to her, such as in the county of Conwy where there is a village called Llansanffraid Glan Conwy (St. Ffraid's Church on the Bank of the Conwy).

Saint Brighid / Bridget makes many appearances, but there

was more than one Saint Brighid in Ireland apparently. The curious thing is that neither Brighid nor Ffraid seem to be connected with metalworking in their many Welsh legends. The nearest that they come to it is Brighid being involved with brewing, while Ffraid is credited with giving a distaff to a ploughman to do duty for his broken mould-board (which could be made either of wood or metal).[33]

Gofannon

Gofannon, the son of Don, is much more the Celtic god we should look to as the blacksmith deity. One of the tasks of the hero Cullwch to win Olwen as his bride was to get the plough of his brother Amaethon sharpened by Gofannon.[34] This is described in the *Mabinogi of Math fab Mathonwy*.[35]

In another fragmentary tale, Gofannon killed Dylan Ail Don, not realising it was his nephew.[36] Versions of his name are found to be venerated as a blacksmith god in Gaul: Gobanos, Gobannus and Cobannus.

The Craig-Y-Don Blacksmith

Here is a brief version of a Welsh fairytale that demonstrates the blacksmith's confidence in dealing with the supernatural:

A blacksmith who lived at Craig-Y-Don was a man with a marvellous thirst to him, which could only be quenched with fine Welsh ale. He must have been especially thirsty one night, because as he staggered home from the pub he saw a lot of tiny little men jump out of the rocks around him. Rubbing his eyes and shaking his head, he could still see them. What's worse, he could hear one talking to him! As he slowly focussed, he heard the little chap say, "If you do not stop living this reckless life, you will soon die! But if you make amends and stay sober, it will be all the better for you."

The blacksmith wanted to ask him what he meant, but as

soon as he said it all the little men were gone, disappeared back into the good grey Welsh rocks. Well, much as he liked fine Welsh ale, he took heed of the fairy's warning, worked hard and no longer visited the pub. A few months later, a stranger to the area brought a horse to be shod. Because he wasn't familiar with the horse and it seemed a little frisky, he tied its halter to the ring of a quenching pot he had fixed to the wall. It was usually full of water to quench hot iron.

As soon as he went around the back of the horse to shoe it, it panicked, reared and pulled its halter, still tied to the pot, off the wall and galloped off. What is more, its rider seemed to have disappeared too. Shaking his head ruefully at the damage, he looked at the hole in the wall where some bricks had been pulled away by the quenching pot. He caught a glint, and when he looked nearer found three brass kettles full of golden coins.[37]

Chapter 5

Scotland

Far fewer of the Gaelic Pagan gods and goddesses have been identified specifically in Scotland, possibly due to the firm influence of Christianity there from early times. In the case of blacksmith gods one can understand the lack of references in a land not blessed with natural deposits of metal, but it is quite possible that the early Gaels shared a similar mythology with Ireland, where many settlers originated from. In the Orkney Islands folk used to get lucky talismans made by the local blacksmith and certainly there was a respect for the ordinary blacksmith (and his strength) as this Gaelic proverb demonstrates:

An uair a théid an gobhainn air bhathal 'se is feàrr a bhi réidh ris.
(When the smith gets wildly excited,'tis best to agree with him.)

The proverb uses the Gaelic word Gobhainn, which together with Gobha are the local terms for a blacksmith. This points towards the possibility that Goibniu was recognised as the blacksmith god here.

I suppose the thing that most readily springs to mind when one mentions "Scotland" and "blacksmith" together is the custom of weddings over the blacksmith's anvil at Gretna Green. Young couples who could not get parental consent in England because they were under 21, and were afraid the church would side with the reluctant parents, could flee over the border to Scotland where the age of marital consent was 16. However, the Scottish Kirk did not approve of this, so blacksmiths and other men at Gretna Green performed a legal "marriage of declaration" until it was outlawed in 1940.

Another Scots custom from the North East of the country is

bathing a child in the iron-rich water of the smithy trough to cure rickets. The child is subsequently laid on the anvil and the tools are passed over him with some suitable words, before a second bath. It all sounds very uncomfortable!

The Horse Riding Witch of Yarrow

Two apprentice blacksmiths who were brothers reportedly had a frightening experience back in the 17th century. One complained that at night a witch would come and put a bridle on him and ride him, transformed into a horse. (Sounds like some erotically kinky dream there!) Anyway, his brother bravely offered to swap beds with him, and the same happened to him. After riding him, the witch tethered him to a tree. Once she had walked away, he struggled and managed to get out of the bridle, and turned back into a young man.

Hiding behind the tree with the bridle, he jumped out and surprised the witch on her return by flinging the bridle onto her. Of course, she turned into a horse, so now he jumped upon her back and rode furiously back to the forge. Being sure to keep the halter on, the two young smiths shoed the horse, and the next morning the witch was found in agony, screaming at the pain of horseshoes nailed into her feet. Needless to say she never returned.

The Smith and the Fairies.

In this old fairytale, the smith has some very unusual visitors. The tale was originally collected by the Rev. Thomas Pattieson of Islay in the late 19th century.[38]

MacEachern the smith of Crossbrig sorrowfully struck his hammer against the piece of metal he working on, but his heart was not in it, and he hit it in the wrong place. Cursing he threw it in the spoil heap. "It is a big spoil heap you are a-getting there!" came a voice from the doorway. "What ails you

Blacksmith MacEachern?" it asked.

The smith turned to the door and recognised the wise old man who stood there. He was seldom seen unless he was needed, and had not visited the village for some time.

"It is not so me that ails, but my son," he explained. The old man had a piercing eye and a way of getting you to say directly what was in your heart.

"He was as fit as any 13-year-old one day, running about, getting into mischief and eating me out of house and home. Yet these last months he has took to his bed, wastes away, sleeps most of the day, and starts to look old beyond his years. There seems nothing I can do to make him better, and I fear he may die."

The old man looked gravely into the forge fire as he listened, and paused before replying. "It would be a shame to deprive the good folk hereabouts of a good blacksmith and his apprentice," he pronounced slowly. "The trouble is, I do not think the one in the bed is your son. I think your son has been taken by Daoine Sith, and they have left a Sibhreach, a changeling, in place of him. There is one way to know for sure – save up all the eggshells you can from you and your good neighbours. Spread them out on the floor where he can see them, and then pour water from a jug into them, two at a time. Carry the full eggshells in pairs as if they were of great weight around the fire."

The smith was mystified, but in desperation was willing to try anything to get his son back in full health again. He went to thank the old man, but he had disappeared as silently as he came. The next day he did all that he had been told, watched by the figure in the bed. He had not got halfway through filling and carrying the eggshells when there was a great guffaw of laughter from the bed as the supposedly sick boy exclaimed, "In eight-hundred years of life I have never seen anything so silly before."

When he retreated downstairs to the forge, the old man was already standing there. He told him what had occurred.

"Aha!" said the old fellow. "Wasn't I right all along? Now you get rid of that lout and I'll bet that your son is in Brorra-cheill in a digh, a well-known hill of the wee folk. Go back upstairs and bank the fire up until it is roaring hot. You'll know how to do that with your trade. When he asks you why, toss him into it. If it is your son (which I very much doubt) he will call out to be saved, but I'm thinking that it is more likely that this thing will fly up out of the roof."

Once again the blacksmith mounted the stairs, bearing lots of extra fuel for the fire, which he piled on.

"What is the use of a fire like that?" asked the invalid.

"You'll see soon," came the smith's grim reply, as he blew it with his bellows until the whole hearth was red hot.

"What an earth are you doing – what is the use of that roaring fire in a small bedroom like this?" was the question.

Without another word the smith's brawn arms had grabbed him from the bed and thrown him in the fire. With a dreadful, piercing shriek, the sibhreach shot up through the smoke hole and was gone. Stunned, the smith returned down stairs to find that the old man had been watching the results of his work from out in the yard, and had witnessed the fiend fly out of the chimney.

Giving him a chance to catch his breath, the old man gave him his final instructions, as matter of fact as if he was telling him to chop wood. As a result, the smith went to the round green hill just outside the village, which most sensible folk gave a wide berth to. With him as instructed for this particular special night he took three items: a Bible (to guard against the wee folk), a dirk of iron they abhorred in shape and metal, and a sleeping cock. As he trod near to the mound he heard tinkling, unearthly music and strange laughter. As he got nearer he could see an opening. Plunging the dirk into the threshold to stop it closing in on him, (since the fae folk hated it) he advanced with his Bible thrust out in front of him like a weapon. Inside, to his surprise he could see his son working away at a forge, under the malevolent gaze of dark, crafty creatures who asked harshly what he wanted there.

"I have come for my son, and will not leave without him," said the smith in a voice that he hoped sounded fiercer and stronger than he felt at that moment. His words seemed to have little worth to the company of furious fairies who faced, but dare not approach him. They cackled with horrible laughter in derision. That dreadful sound woke the sleeping cock in the smith's tool bag, which crowed loudly and repeatedly, thinking it had missed the dawn. As a race that lives purely by night it was a hateful sound to the fairies, and in horror they pushed the son and his father, the cock and Bible out of their world. The smith remembered to pick up the dirk as they stumbled out, so that the hill closed and they could not be followed.

The father was overjoyed to have his son back, but the lad was clearly shocked and confused at what had happened to him. Gradually, he started to eat a little more heartily, the colour did return to his white cheeks, and he started to take an interest on what was going on around him again. Yet he hardly said a word, as if the horror of what had happened was a thing he did not want to describe. His father (and the old man occasionally) watched him patiently, letting him take his own time to recover.

That took place a whole year and a day later when the smith was working on a sword on for a local chieftain. Suddenly the son, who had been watching said, "That is not the best way to do it, here let me!" The smith was so stunned that he stood back and let the young man take up his tools and go to work in a way that he would never have thought possible. The sword was a masterpiece of the metalworkers' craft, much admired for its balance, cutting ability and decoration, and became known as *Claidheamh Ceann-Ileach*.[39]

Nothing like it had been seen before, and soon there was a stream of good customers to the forge wanting similar weapons, not just to fight with, but to be displayed as fine ornaments to their best costumes. Father and son worked steadily together in harmony, earning good money and happy in their chosen craft. They never saw the old man again at the forge, but maybe you might. Caonis gall is close to the church at Kilchoman, Islay.

Chapter 6

Mainland Europe

Poland

Svarog

Svarog is the Slavic god of fire and blacksmithing, but has also been worshipped as the supreme deity. From the 15th century *Hypatian Codex*, derived from a Slavic translation of a 6th century Russian manuscript, we find that:

> *[Then] began his reign Feosta (Hephaestus), whom the Egyptians called Svarog ... during his rule, from the heavens fell the smith's prongs and weapons were forged for the first time; before that, [people] fought with clubs and stones. Feosta also commanded the women that they should have only a single husband – and that is why Egyptians called him Svarog. After him ruled his son, his name was the Sun, and they called him Dažbog – Sun tsar, son of Svarog, this is Dažbog.*

So it appears that this Svarog was worshipped in some form by the Egyptians as well. Of course we have already met the Greek smith god Hephaestus, here referred to by an alternative name, in Chapter 1 and the classical sources. One source says that "fire was so sacred that it was forbidden to shout or swear whilst it was being lit" and that folklore describes him as a winged dragon breathing fire. He is associated with "a golden horned ox, boar, horse and falcon (called Varagna) and he can also shape shift into the wind."[40]

The Story of the Sleeping Knights

A stranger came to a blacksmith and offered a big reward if he could do a job for him and keep it secret. The blacksmith agreed, and was given a gold bar and instructed to make a horseshoe from it. The stranger then led him on a long walk to a secret hidden cave in Koscieliska Valley.

Inside were a horde of sleeping knights in armour with axes and spears. There were also sleeping horses with more golden horseshoes like the one the smith had made. He was asked to fix his horseshoe to a marvellous stallion, and he did so without it even waking. Despite wanting to know many things, all his mysterious host would tell him was that they had been waiting centuries for a great battle in which they would be needed. Thunder would summon them and earth would quake to arouse them to defend Poland.

Finally the smith was led back to his village and given a great bag of gold, and made to promise that he would keep the secret of the cave, its occupants and the job he had done. Unfortunately, like many smiths who enjoy talking to the visitors who sought warmth and company at his forge, he broke his word, and immediately the coins in the bag turned to sand, and the smith could never find the cave again.

Romania and the Roma

Romanian male gypsies often act as smiths, with their wives being famed for divination and interpreting dreams and omens. They are thought to be able to work together to invoke spirits of the air and wind.

The Roma people have, like many of their fellow gypsy races, been badly victimised to this day; one of their own stories explains why this is:[41]

When the Roman soldiers were going to crucify Jesus, they ordered four nails from a blacksmith. Knowing what they would be used for he refused and was killed on the spot. A second blacksmith was called, but as he was making the second of the nails he heard a voice telling not to, because the intended victim was innocent. He was also killed when he refused to finish the job, so only two nails were completed. The soldiers then found a gypsy blacksmith who had recently arrived in Jerusalem. He was told to make the remaining two nails, but the voices of the two dead blacksmiths came to him, imploring him not to do it. The soldiers were returning, and the spirits left. He tried to quench the last nail with water, but it stayed burning blood red for a long time. Frightened, he took down his tent and fled, condemned for his action with his descendants to wander forever. The soldiers found the one nail he had finished, so only had three for the crucifixion.

The custom of smiths not working on Good Friday in memory of the use of nails on that day has been recorded in some countries, including England, at Skegness.

Spain

The Snake of Aralar

The snake in question is more of a horrific flying serpent spirit, sometimes credited with having seven heads. It is called the Herensuge and allegedly lived in a large number of places, so maybe there was a family of them? Apparently it flew through the air making a buzzing noise and lived both on human and cattle meat. Heroes from various regions claimed to have killed it. One of those was an un-named blacksmith from Mondragón who heated up a bar of metal to red hot in his forge then plunged it into the monster. Other versions have it poisoned, set on fire or having its head cut off by an angel.

France

Whilst most of France was likely to share its blacksmith gods with other Celtic / Briton cultures, the area around Gaul had

Belisama. Almost uniquely, this blacksmith deity is a goddess rather than a god.

Siberia

Siberia and the Yakut region have the enigmatic demon K'daai as their metalworking and fire spirit.

Russia

In some areas of Russia, including Mingrelia, the Caucasus and some neighbouring regions, blacksmiths have a reputation as magicians, and oaths are taken on the anvil rather than the Bible. The Caucasus mountain region (between Europe and Asia near to the Caspian Sea) has a blacksmith god called variously Kurdalaegon, Ossetian or Kurdaligon.[42] There are a couple of fine blacksmith stories from Russia I would like to pass on.

The Blacksmith and the Demon[43]

Churches used to be a lot more colourful than they are today with coloured pictures on the walls to illustrate the stories the priests told, for people who very often could not read for themselves. A good blacksmith went to such a church with his smart six-year-old son, and was very impressed with a picture of a demon at the Last Judgement. It was black and red with a pointed tail, horns and hooves and looked very frightening.

As he walked home, an idea came to him to have a similar picture painted on the door of his smithy, so he found the same artist who had painted at the church and paid him to make a similar picture for him. Then each morning when he entered to start work he would greet the picture with, "Good morning fellow countryman," or, "How are you today sir?" and hoped that this would keep him on the right side of the real demon if he was about. This carried on for about ten years until he died, and his son took over.

He did not think much of greeting the demon each morning. Why his father should have such an ugly picture he did not know, but people were used to it now, so he couldn't really do away with it. He thought if he gradually wore it away, that would give him a good excuse, so he started each morning by showing his contempt for the demon by hitting the picture sharply three times with his hammer. When he went to church he would gladly light a tapering candle for a saint's day, but he would spit in the face of the demon of the wall painting when no one was looking. This went on for three long years, and the real demon (who felt the hurt done to the pictures) was rubbing his sore head and thought that he would have to do something to stop it.

The demon changed himself into the form of a strong young man, and went to the forge to offer his services. "In exchange for being your apprentice I can carry water from the well, blow the bellows, clean up and carry goods for your customers," he offered smilingly. The blacksmith liked the sound of that, so the deal was agreed, and the demon set to learning all he could about being a blacksmith. He was such a fast learner that in a month the smith could trust him to do anything that he could do, and started to take the occasional time off and let him get on with it.

It was on such a day when the young man was left by himself at the smithy, and the blacksmith off for a lunchtime drink at the tavern, when an old lady came riding along in her carriage. Running alongside he shouted, "We can do you a service madam. We can change old folks into young!" The lady commanded her coachman to stop and got out. She was not convinced, but was willing to see what was being offered.

"Can you really do it?" she asked.

"Oh yes," was the confident reply. "If we did not know how to do it we would be fools for offering it. The fee is 500 roubles."

She gave him the money, and he took some of it outside to the coachman and said, "You are to go into the village and buy two buckets of milk, and bring them back here carefully, not spilling a drop." The coachman obeyed.

With him out of the way, for a long while hopefully, he grabbed the old lady's feet with his tongs and dropped her into the furnace fire. She screamed a bit, but was quickly burnt up until only her bones were left. When the coachman returned with the two buckets of milk, he emptied them into a tub and tossed the bones in too. There was a bubbling, then after a minute or two the lady emerged from the milk alive, young, beautiful and new. She hardly noticed that her clothes were gone until her embarrassed coachman flung his cloak around her and took her straight home to her husband.

The lord hardly recognised his wife until she spoke. He stood there with his mouth open. "You had better go and get yourself made young at the forge like me," his wife commanded. "Now I am young and beautiful I do not want to be seen with an old man like you! Go now and give the man 500 roubles."

By the time her husband had got over his shock and got to the forge, the blacksmith had got back from the tavern. His apprentice was nowhere to be seen, so he had started work by himself by the time the lord got there.

"You must make a new man of me," said the lord, "at once!"

"How on earth could I manage to do that?" asked the blacksmith, thinking the lord was going silly in his old age.

"You know perfectly well how – you did it for her ladyship," came the indignant reply. "She wants nothing to do with me unless I become young as well."

"But I haven't seen her ladyship today, so how could I have made her young? I have no idea how to do it."

The coachman whispered deferentially into his lord's ear, who coughed then carried on: "He says it was your apprentice, but that is just the same. If the apprentice knows how to do it he must have learnt it off you, so get on with it man or you'll feel the birch across your back!"

The frightened blacksmith had no doubt that the lord meant what he said. He was the law in these parts, with a lot of power.

In desperation he conferred with the coachman to see what he knew about what had happened to her ladyship.

"Alright, I will do the same as my apprentice, and hope it works. If not no doubt I will suffer for it anyway," complained the smith, once more looking in vain for his apprentice out through the doorway.

He repeated the process just as the coachman told him, with some added clues from what the lady had told the lord. He sent the coachman off for more milk from the village. He stripped the lord naked, picked him up with his tongs and dropped him in the fire. As he blew on the bellows the lord was quickly burnt to a cinder. Quickly raking out the bones, he dropped them into a tub of milk and waited. And waited. And waited some more, but after an hour nothing had happened. The smith was beside himself and then the lady sent a messenger to the smithy to see that all was going well. He had to admit that all he had was the lord's bones in a tub of milk.

Word soon got back to her, and in a fury she sent her men to seize the unhappy blacksmith and hang him, since he had admitted killing her lord. As they bound his hands to take him to the gallows, the young apprentice re-appeared.

"What's going on?" he asked so innocently. "Where are they taking you?"

"To the gallows!" cried his master. Crying, he described all that had happened.

"If you promise not to hurt the picture anymore, and treat it nice like your father, then the lord will be alive once more, and younger too in the bargain."

"Yes, yes, I swear by my anvil and all the saints I will do as you say," promised the blacksmith.

"Wait there a moment," commanded the young man to the servants, going into the smithy. In moments he had returned with the lord, looking no more than 20 years old (although he had mercifully put his old clothes back on).

"Look! Here is your master," proclaimed the young man, "now let that blacksmith free."

They did as he said, and the blacksmith kept his promise, never neglecting to wish a good morning to the demon picture. The young man was not seen again, but I hear that the lord and lady had three more children in the next few years, and looked very well on it.

One-Eyed Likho[44]

Smiths can be thoughtful fellows, and one got to thinking that with his honourable occupation and happy customers who always paid their bills, he had never really encountered evil, who is known there as One-Eyed Likho. He started by going for a good drink at the tavern, since he had heard that drink was often the root of all evil, but he found none there, so, like me, thought it was a lie.

So he set off down the road and came upon a tailor. As they walked and talked together, he told him of his plan. "That sounds an interesting plan," said the tailor. "Like you, I have never encountered Likho either. Would you mind if I joined you?"

"That would be splendid," said the blacksmith. "Two heads are better than one."

Just then they came to a dark path branching off the main road, covered over with trees. It looked as if it could be more interesting than the main road they both knew, so they wandered down it. It became narrower, but they still pressed onwards. By the time they reached the end of it, night had fallen, but they could see a rundown cottage.

"Let us see if we can stay there the night," suggested the blacksmith.

He knocked boldly on the door. Nobody came, and so they thought it might be empty. The door opened easily, so they went inside. It was dirty and squalid, with broken down chairs and rubbish around the floor. They sat down on a dusty box, and were just wondering what to do, when a voice behind them made them jump.

"Good evening visitors!" came the voice of a very tall woman with a crooked back, matted hair and but a single eye to peer out of.

"Good evening Grandmother," replied the tailor. "May we stop the night here with you please?"

"Oh yes, you are very welcome. I am hungry for a meal, so let me just build up the fire." With that the woman scuttled out of the door to return quickly with firewood which was soon roaring away in the hearth. Then without saying anything else she grabbed the tailor, cut his throat from ear to ear and shoved him in the oven that was heated by the fire. The blacksmith was terrified, but could not escape, as she was between him and the door. How could he save his own life? She was sure to want to eat him as well!

It seemed an age whilst with her one eye staring at him she took the cooked tailor from the oven and ate him, limb by limb, with his gravy running down her chin.

"Grandmother, I am a blacksmith," he said nervously.

"Oh yes, what can you forge?"

"Almost anything," replied the blacksmith truthfully.

"Then make me an eye!" called the woman, challenging him.

"Well I could, but I'd need to keep you very still while I hammered it in," he said in a matter-of-fact way.

She went and fetched two pieces of grubby cord, one thick

and one thin. She was suspicious, and gave him the thinnest to bind her with.

"Now turn over, Grandmother," he instructed. As she did, the thin cord broke. "That will not do Grandmother," he complained, so he bound her tightly with the thicker cord instead. "Now try that and turn over," he said. But however she turned, squirmed or twisted, she could hardly move. Without a word the blacksmith heated up his awl in the blazing fire, and when it glowed he plunged it into her one good eye, hammering it in.

"Agghh you miserable villain!" she screamed. "I cannot see, but I'll have you yet!"

She was still blocking the door with her tall form, and her long nailed hands grabbed at the air in front of her. Soon there was a baa-ing from the door, and her few sheep made their way in for the night between her legs. There was even more blocking of the way to prevent blacksmith from getting out now, and he shivered the night in the corner, afraid to fall asleep.

In the morning the sheep made their way out again. Quick as a hammer blow but twice as quietly, he turned his sheepskin blanket inside out, so that the fur was on the outside. He put his arms through the holes and crawled out through the woman's legs, trying to baa convincingly. She was shoving the sheep out one at a time after checking the fleece on their backs, and she treated him just the same in her blindness.

As soon as blacksmith was outside he got to his feet and yelled defiantly "Hah! Likho, you do much evil but you will not have me!" and ran towards the little wooded path.

"I have not done with you yet, you wretch!" shouted Likho after him.

As the blacksmith hurried through the wood he saw something glinting in the sunshine that filtered through a gap in the leaves. It was a golden axe, driven into the side of a tree, the like of which he had never seen before. As his hand grasped it though, it stuck fast to it, and he could not escape. Behind him he could hear Likho crashing through the wood catching him up. If she found him she was bound to eat him now, and he thought back to his village, and what a farmer had once told him of a rat escaping from a trap in his barn. There was nothing for it – with his free hand he got the sharp knife which he always carried on his belt, and hardly bearing to look desperately cut through the wrist of the hand stuck to the axe. Wrapping his bloody stump into his shirt, he ran as fast as he could back to the village, where his injury was tended to. Ever after he would use the stump as a warning to people: "That lost hand is the result of evil, and proof that I met Likho herself, who ate my friend the tailor completely."

Whether that last tale has a connection with lame gods or even Lugh of the Silver Hand or Tiw / Tyr is impossible to discern, but personally I put it down to coincidence. The moral certainly is in no doubt: if you look for evil you will find it.

Chapter 7

Finland and Scandinavia

Finland

Although thought originally to be an air spirit, the immortal Seppo Ilmarinen the "Eternal Hammerer" is a very famous blacksmith in Finnish mythology. Seppo is a boy's name synonymous with "smith".

He forged the Sampo Mill of Fortune, which would bring good luck to anyone who owned it. Unfortunately it was captured in a battle and destroyed. He made it to gain a wife who was the daughter of Louhi. Sadly she was killed by Kullervo, and a second daughter was refused him, but he carried her off anyway. She turned out to have disgusting behaviour, so he turned her into a seagull. Sounds like a lot of trouble for nothing![57]

After all that, Ilmarinen tried to get the Sampo back from Louhi, aided by Väinämöinen and Lemminkäinen. They failed, and Louhi captured the sun and moon in retaliation. Ilmarinen made new ones (is there no end to his talents?) but they were not as good as the originals, so he managed to trick Louhi into letting them go again.

Seppo Ilmarinen is also held responsible for creating the dome of the sky, a woman out of silver and gold, and a kantele musical instrument. He is said to be able to work with any metal. Some scholars believe that Sampo / Sempo and the sky are actually the same thing.[58]

There is confusion between Ilmarinen (also known as Ilmorinen and Ilmollini) and another deity known as Inmar, whose name means sky, which he is also credited with creating. Inmar is invoked for aid in various Finnish rune songs.

As elsewhere, blacksmiths are revered in Finland and given

gifts of brandy. There is a Finnish proverb saying: *"Fine bread always for the smith, and dainty morsels for the hammerer."*

The *Kalvalla*[59] is a major source of Finnish mythology. In the epic poem Ilmarinen is described as inventing and making both military weapons and practical tools to the highest of standards.

> *Came to earth to work the metal;*
> *He was born upon the coal-mount,*
> *Skilled and nurtured in the coal-fields;*
> *In one hand a copper hammer,*
> *In the other tongs of iron;*
> *In the night was born the blacksmith,*
> *In the morn he built his smithy;*
> *Sought with care a favoured hillock,*
> *Where the winds might fill his bellows;*
> *Found a hillock in the swamp-land,*
> *Where the iron hid abundant,*
> *There he built his smelting-furnace.*

Much of Finland's mythology has survived in rune songs, which were still sung up to about a century ago. Fortunately, many were collected, and from them we get:

> *He's a smith extraordinary, the most skilful of all craftsmen, Who hammered out the vault of heaven, Forged the sky-lid there above us Without leaving mark of hammer Or a trace of tongs upon it.*[60]
>
> *Ilmarinen had been born, Born and grown to manhood too, Born upon a hill of charcoal, Grew up on a cindery heathland, In one hand a copper hammer, In the other his tiny tongs.*[61]

There are also a large body of traditional folk songs, sung specifically by boys, girls, men, women or mixed groups. From a very lengthy one preserved in the Kantelar collection (3.6) called *The Ballad of the Virgin Mary* we find in one verse the words:

Here the blacksmiths are forging
The demons' smiths are clanging,
He went to the smiths' workshop;
"What are the smiths forging
The demons' smiths hammering?"
That cruel Judas
Worst of evil boys
And basest of father's sons
Uttered a word and spoke to him thus:
"I forge a chain for the Creator
And a shackle rope for God.
But I forgot to measure
How thick the Creator's neck
How thick and how long it is
And how wide across."
So the famous son of God
Put this into words;
"The Creator's neck is thick
As thick as long
And as wide across
As your own neck is."[62]

Make of those puzzling lines what you may, but they really need to be put into the context of a song that takes up 26 pages in the source book!

Finland is sometimes associated with the rest of Scandinavia due to their geographic proximity, but in fact their cultures and languages are entirely different. The main Finnish language is Uralic and is spoken in a part of Norway, but has more in common with the language of Estonia and a part of Russia. In contrast, Scandinavian countries such as Denmark, Norway, Iceland, Faeroes and Sweden share Germanic language and cultural roots.

Scandinavia

Dwarves

Smithing is not exclusively the domain of demi-gods or men within the Norse mythology. Several dwarves put in an appearance, both as the teachers of smiths such as Wayland, or craftsmen in their own right, sometimes working on commissions for the gods. In the creation myth they are described as maggots in the body of the creator giant Ymir. Think for instance of the four dwarves, Dvallin, Alfrik, Berling and Grer, who created the magical Brisingamen necklace of great power. Freya so much wanted it that she agreed the price demanded, to spend a night in bed with each of them.

The necklace leads to much trouble later when it is stolen from her. What type of magic it is associated with is never explicit, but female figures sometimes identified as possible priestesses are often shown with elaborate necklaces or neck torcs in several cultures. There is a Viking Era silver pendant artefact believed to represent Freyja with a necklace in the Stockholm Museum. It was found in Aska, Sweden.[63]

The two dwarf brothers Brokkr and Eitri are credited with the manufacture of Gungnir, Odin's spear, and a boar with golden bristles called Gullinbursti, after accepting a wager from the trickster god Loki. They also made Draupnir a ring that produced eight more rings every nine nights, very similar to the cursed ring Andvarenaut. Most importantly they manufactured Mjollnir, Thor's mighty war hammer.[64]

It is worth mentioning in the context of this book that although Thor has a hammer (which magically returns to his hand after being thrown) he uses it to fight with, rather than work with metal. No anvil or forge is associated with him in original stories, and I believe later writers who have included blacksmith in his attributes are mistaken. He is more of a fertility god, associated with good harvests. His phallic shaped hammer (with its shortened handle caused by the sabotage of Loki in its creation) is used to lay in the lap of a bride at a wedding and bless horns of mead within the myths. He does throw thunderbolts in some tales, something associated with some other smith gods, but he may not have necessarily have made them. He also has a belt megingjörð (power-belt) and the iron gauntlets Járngreipr to increase his strength, given to him by a giantess Grid, but it is not said where she got them from.

Dain the dwarf was the forger of the cursed sword Dainsleif. It had to kill someone before being sheathed. In another tale Dain the dwarf and his brother Nabbi made a magical boar called Hildisvini.

Regin

Regin, the son of Hreidmar, was a legendary blacksmith in Denmark. He had a foster son called Sigurd (or Siegfried) and two brothers called Otr and Fafnir. Poor old Fafnir got turned into a dragon through a cursed ring called Andvarenaut. Regin started to come under the curse of the ring too, so Sigurd set out to kill Fafnir, armed with a sword forged by Regin out of the fragments of one owned by Sigurd's real father. Sigurd succeeded in killing Fafnir with the sword, and cooked his heart to eat so that it would give him extra strength. When he licked a thumb with the gravy of Fafnir on it, he found to his astonishment that he could understand what the birds were saying. The message was not pretty: the birds were saying that far from being grateful, Regin planned to kill Sigurd, but forewarned, Sigurd killed Regin first. He then took Fafnir's treasure, which including the cursed ring which he unknowingly put onto his own finger.

Sigmund / Siegfried drew a special sword called Glam (grief)[65] from a huge oak pillar called Barnstokk in one story. It has been thrust into it by the god Odin, and the hero is the only one who can obtain it, which has similarities to the Arthurian sword in the stone tale in Chapter 4.

Coming to a castle Siegfried leapt through flames to reach the beautiful warrior maiden Brunhilde who had been put into a deep sleep by Odin. He awoke her with a kiss and gave her the ring as a promise that he would be back to marry her. The ring's curse took effect again, and after being given a drugged drink he married Princess Gudrun (or Kriemhild) and forgot Brunhilde. No doubt some readers will recognise some parts of this story from Wagner's operas.

The Norwegian runic poem refers to Regin against the Ræið rune: *"Riding they say is horses work: Reginn forged of swords the finest."*[66]

Crossley-Holland[67] makes the point that although the myth is transmitted in Scandinavian myths, it actually takes place in a Germanic setting, by the River Rhine, and the land occupied by the Franks.

The Doppelgänger and the Blacksmith

Keightley[68] relates a blacksmith legend from Denmark: a blacksmith attacks with a hot iron a troll who is kidnapping a pregnant woman. The troll drops his captive, who is taken to recover at the forge. The shock results in her giving birth to twins almost straight away. Leaving her there he goes to find her husband, but is surprised to find him in bed with a creature that appears to him to be his wife. It is the husband's turn to be amazed when the blacksmith recognises the monster for what it is and kills it.

Völundr

The Old Norse stories sometimes call Wayland Smith by an earlier name, Völundr. As such he appears in the poem *Völundarkviða*, from the *Poetic Edda*[69], in which the tale with King Nidud is told, but also that of his swan maiden wife. Inevitably there are several versions of the story of how he came by this wife, complicated by a 19th century reworking of the themes by

Wagner in his operas when he makes Völundr the creator of the fateful ring in his *Der Ring des Nibelungen* (*The Ring of the Nibelung*)[70] based on the *Völsunga saga*[71] and *The Nibelungenlied*.[72] For a retelling of the story of the encounters with King Niduð, see the English Anglo Saxon retelling, (Chapter 3) but the Norse version has the princess going to Völundr with the ring of his wife (which has been stolen from him) to be mended rather than her going to receive jewellery he has made for her. Also Niduð takes his fine sword and wears it. Völundr is also credited with creating a labyrinth for King Niduð, giving rise to an Icelandic habit of calling a maze or a labyrinth "Völund's House".[73] (A labyrinth has only one convoluted pathway, but a maze has multiple choices of route, only one of which will lead to the exit.)

In the Greek myth, Daedalus is associated with a labyrinth of the Minotaur on Crete, and makes wings to escape, so maybe there is some parallel going on there. The tale is also referred to in *Þiðrekssaga* (as well as the Anglo Saxon sources) and places Niðud as a king in Sweden.[74] Völundr himself is credited with being of Finnish origin in some Norse sources. This may be significant as, in some of the sagas, Lapp magicians are brought in as respected foreign experts in a magic different to that of the native peoples. It would be the modern equivalent of bringing in a foreign Voodoo doctor to combat an English witch.

Völundr and his two brothers Egil and Slagfiðr come across three swan maidens bathing in the river Rhine, who have taken their suits of feathers off. They have in some analysis been associated with Valkyries, gatherers of the valiant slain of battlefields. The brothers take the suits, and the maidens Olrún, Hervör and Haðguðr agree to live with them for nine years. At the end of that period they leave, and two brothers go off on adventures together, but Völundr stays behind and looks for his lost wife Hervör. She leaves him a ring, which he makes 700 copies of. Why we do not know.

Völundr is also referenced in the *Þiðrekssaga* where he makes a gift of the magical sword Miming. The sword is said to be so sharp that in a duel with another blacksmith, Amilias, he takes a diagonal blow at his shoulder. Amilias believes he has been saved by his strong armour, until asked to shake himself. He falls into two diagonally cut pieces!

Vadi is the alleged father of Völundr, but his ancestry is very confused and contradictory, with competing sources for his birth. There is some inference that he was of Finnish extraction, an attribute that would associate him with magic that the Norse people admired as powerful. He seems to be part human, (capable of being harmed by another human) and part god (magical powers), so I have classed him as a demi-god. What is generally agreed is that he was taught by Mimir and two dwarves. The dwarves aim to kill him for learning too much, but he gets to them first.

There are a few ancient illustrations of Wayland / Völundr: the front panel of the Northumbrian Franks Casket (made of whalebone in the 8th century) shows him holding a skull with pincers that he is fashioning into a cup. A headless corpse lies at his feet. The casket is in the British Museum.[75]

An 8th-9th century picture stone (Number 8) from Ardre, Gotland, Sweden, shows him flying away as an eagle leaving Niðhad's daughter and her two dead brothers behind.

That eagle image is repeated again in a recent discovery of a beautiful 10th century copper alloy with silver gilding brooch from Uppakra, Sweden.

Chapter 8

Christian Saints and Sources

Behold, I have created the smith that bloweth the coals in the fire, and that bringeth forth an instrument for his work; and I have created the waster to destroy.
The Bible, King James Edition, Isiah 54.16

I have in the main tried to keep Christian saints and sources separate to the geographic chapters in which they could have appeared. This is partly because many of the saints cover several countries, and would have involved a lot of repetition if I had dealt with them geographically. Obviously Biblical references cover all Christian communities around the world.

I would say as a Pagan that I have great respect for the Bible in parts as an historical document, and in parts as a good guide for many people to live their lives by. However, even Christian theologians and academics admit that some parts of it appear to be in error, or have maybe become distorted through being carried orally for several generations before being committed to writing, particularly within the Old Testament. This is not unusual, and has happened to most ancient religious texts of the world's many religions. That does inevitably mean that part of the writings and ideas may be regarded as mythology or legends in their own right. I do not say that to be offensive, merely accurate and practical. My first figure is a case in point.

Tubal Cain
In the Christian Bible, this descendant of Cain and son of Lamech and Zillah is said to be a *"forger of all instruments of bronze and iron."*[45]

In writing about the first tools (replacing stone and wood) the text must have been written after the Iron Age had started, which makes it rather anomalous for dating in the context of much of the other material, which is believed by many to date from circa 1446 BCE.[46] That does not detract from the smith story within the Bible, but does inform it. Tubal Cain was said to marry Nin-Banda and have two sons, Ham and Japhet, who presumably followed their father's business and who, according to modern research, are not the sons of Noah.

Incidentally Tubal Cain features within Freemason ritual, being part of the greeting of a 3rd degree Master Mason and the name of the associated secret handshake. The Masons do possess several complex theories as to the meaning and origin of his name, and how it relates to other gods such as Vulcan, which can be found online.[47] The symbol for this degree is two ball and cane (a pun on the name) surrounded by another two ball and cane.

There is also an early Jewish source that says:

But Tubal, one of his children by the other wife, exceeded all men in strength, and was very expert and famous in martial performances. He procured what tended to the pleasures of the body by that method; and first of all invented the art of making brass.[48]

The Clan of Tubal Cain

This is the name of an important late witchcraft group.[49] Their origins were with the controversial Robert Cochrane (real name Roy Bowers, 1931-66) in Windsor and his successor Evan John Jones. Many of his teachings are contained within a number of published letters.[50]

The connection with Tubal Cain is made by the "Pillars of Tubal Cain", which were alleged to be inscribed by Cain's family to preserve their knowledge beyond the ravages of the great flood that was predicted. For a modern interpretation of this refer to the book by Jackson and Howard.[51]

The Clan of Tubal Cain (also known as the People of Goda)

continues to operate. They are a closed initiatory group claiming a pre-Gardnerian traditional witchcraft heritage, and have also included many high-profile witches and Pagans as associates or within their ranks. The tradition also spread to the USA via Joseph Wilson as the 1734 Tradition, and also spawned the Regency Tradition within the UK.

The Book of Enoch

The Jewish *Book of Enoch* (great grandfather of Noah) is part of the *Apocrypha* i.e. a book not included in the set of manuscripts that were agreed to form the Bible, but associated with it. Some independent Orthodox religious groups accept it as an inspired work, and it was probably composed in around 300 BCE. Fragments of it were found with the Dead Sea Scrolls. The only complete version is in the Ge'ez language, but parts are preserved in Aramaic, Greek and Latin.

In the section Book of Watchers, sin is said to derive from fallen angels who come to earth to take human brides, and made them pregnant. One of them is said to be Azazel who:

... taught men to make swords and knives, and shields, and breastplates, and made known to them the metals and the art of working them, and bracelets and ornaments ...

It is possible that the early church hierarchy would have found it awkward having two contradictory versions of the first blacksmith, in that this is very different from Tubal Cain.

Saint Clement

Saint Clement is technically the patron saint of farriers, rather than all smiths. It has been suggested that he was a Roman bishop who was martyred on 23rd November, 100 CE, by being tied to an anchor and dropped into the sea. There are records of blacksmith apprentices from Woolwich dockyards having an evening parade on his festival, with one of them dressed as St. Clement who made a speech:

> *I am the real Saint Clement, the first founder of brass, iron, and steel from the ore. I have been to Mount Etna, where the god Vulcan first built his forge, and forged the armour and thunderbolts for the god Jupiter.*

Burwash in the Wealdon area also had a feast for blacksmiths where "Old Clem" reputedly stands over the pub doorway.[52] St Clements seems to have been adopted by Christian Danes, with churches dedicated to him including St Clements Danes in the Strand, London. St. Clement is the patron saint of the Worshipful Company of Blacksmiths in the City of London.

Saint Eloy / Eligius / Loye

This saint is also sometimes seen as the guardian of smiths, which seems quite appropriate as he was apprenticed to a goldsmith of Limoges. His festival is on December 1st. From one folk tale he did not always work in gold: he had to shoe a lively horse that would not stand still. He cut off the leg, affixed the shoe and after making the sign of the cross put the leg back on again! He was the patron saint of a 13th century trade guild of blacksmiths in the City of London.

Saint Dunstan

The most colourful legend about this saint (who died in 988 CE) is that the Devil was annoyed at the healing properties of a spring at Tunbridge Wells and poked his nose right below the surface, causing it to go red and taste of sulphur. St. Dunstan pulled him out by the nose using his blacksmith's tongs, which are displayed at Mayfield Convent. Ford[53] tells us that he repeated the trick at the forge another time, when the Devil disguised himself as a beautiful young girl to tempt him. He wouldn't look up from his work, and eventually spotted the hooves beneath the dress, the Devil usually being careless not to transform them. Dunstan clamped his red hot tongs on to the nose of the Devil, who screamed very loud and had to unfurl his wings to escape into the sky.

His 10th century stories mostly relate to his time at the Glastonbury forge. Apparently before being converted to Christianity by St. Alphege, he was alleged to have been a magician involved in occult works and ejected from the king's court.[54] St Dunstan's Day is on May 19th. In one tale he nails horseshoes to the Devil's hooves (he forgot to hide them again!) and would not remove them until Old Nick promised to stay away from farriers. Of course he broke the promise, as you will see elsewhere in this book, but after all he is the Devil.

Saint Boris

Saint Boris appears as the Russian blacksmith saint.[55] He is credited, with Saint Gleb, of producing the first plough. They were martyred in 1015, although some think they were an earlier cult that became Christianised. The original plough was of an enormous size, and they used 12 golden hammers to create it. (I'm not surprised – gold is quite soft so you would soon bend them out of shape.)

Saint Finbar

Saint Finbar is more usually known as the patron saint of Cork, in Ireland, where the cathedral is named after him, but his father Amergin was a 6th century blacksmith who eloped with a high-born local lady.

The enraged local chieftain chased and caught them, and was to burn them at the stake when Finbar's voice was heard from the womb, pleading for his parents and him to be saved, and so they were, as God quenched the flames. Finbar learnt to be a smith from his father, but went on to become a successful evangelist.

The Legend of the Brass Teapot

Legends are sometimes constructed in and around some actual facts, so this story throws up some interesting connections. There are several varying versions of it, which is not surprising if the statement by the influential Victorian occult Theosophical Society is true, that it was from folklore current with the crucifixion.

The brass teapot was supposed to be made from the silver paid to Judas Iscariot for his betrayal of Jesus, therefore becoming mystically endowed. It was made by a blacksmith when Jesus was brought in front of Pontius Pilate, who condemned him.

Judas, overcome with remorse, ran through the streets and tossed the 30 shekels of silver into a smith's vessel to destroy them in the molten metal and not taint other people. The smith was casting a brass pot for a foreign customer. Judas continued running, until he found a place to commit suicide.

The molten metal, a mixture of brass and silver, was made into an intricately engraved pot and sent to King Magdala, near the Sea of Galilee. He recognised its special powers and had it moved to Damascus where it could be kept more securely.

That is the basic tale (subject to regional variations) but consider some of the information that researchers have unearthed since:

- Shekels from Tyre were the only currency recognised by the temple at Jerusalem, and could have possibly come from Pilate's stock of money for local, rather than Roman, use.
- In contradiction, the Bible reported that guards saw him throw the coins away into a field where they were retrieved by others.
- Forgers in the city were known to use unknown combinations of metals together, so adding silver to brass is not such an outlandish idea.
- The brass teapot is referred to as a "grail" in a work by

Christien De Troyes, which in Old French *graal* usually means a broad dish or salver. The Grail of legend has been described in all sorts of forms, with no single definitive description, but including a teapot!

So, are we getting too far off blacksmiths and delving into the turgid world of Grail speculation and mystery? I hope not, since this chapter is supposed to be about Christian saints and sources. So let us close with two biblical quotations:

And He shall sit as a refiner and purifier of silver (Malachi 3:3)

A silversmith will tell you that if silver is allowed to refine for too long it spoils, but if it is refined correctly, you can see yourself in it. In this next passage from another book of the Bible we actually get God saying that He will act as a smith to purge the dross and purify it in fire:

Then the word of the Lord came to me: "Son of man, the people of Israel have become dross to me; all of them are the copper, tin, iron and lead left inside a furnace. They are but the dross of silver. Therefore this is what the Sovereign Lord says: 'Because you have all become dross, I will gather you into Jerusalem. As silver, copper, iron, lead and tin are gathered into a furnace to be melted with a fiery blast, so will I gather you in my anger and my wrath and put you inside the city and melt you. I will gather you and I will blow on you with my fiery wrath, and you will be melted inside her. As silver is melted in a furnace, so you will be melted inside her, and you will know that I the Lord have poured out my wrath on you.'"
(Ezekiel 22)

Inevitably the Gods of one religion are demonised by its successor. Although some of the saint's stories have a smattering of earlier beliefs within them, I feel that it is good that these stories have survived at all, alongside the more formalised, approved texts of the Christian Church. Let us conclude this chapter with a charming Christian inspired folktale.

The Master Smith Story

A smith had made a bargain with the Devil that he should be master of all the trades for seven years, but that after that the Devil should have him, and both had signed the contract. He had put up a sign that read, "Here dwells the Master over all Masters."

The Lord and Saint Peter were wandering the earth and saw it, so they went in.

"Who are you?" said the smith not recognising them. "Read what's over the door if you want to know who I am," he boasted. Just then a man came in with a horse to be shod.

"May I do it?" asked the Lord.

Surprised, the smith gruffly replied he supposed that it would be alright. "I'd hope you do not make such a mess of it that I cannot fix it," he laughed.

The Lord went outside and took one leg off the horse, and placed it into the furnace. He made a shoe and turned its ends up and fixed it to the hoof red hot. Then he filed down the nail heads and clenched the points. Finally he put the leg back on the horse. The smith gazed on amazed, his jaw open and frozen by astonishment into inaction. He continued to watch whilst the Lord repeated the process for the other three legs.

Finally he found his voice and said, "Oh, so you are not such a bad smith after all!" in the biggest of understatements.

"Oh, that is what you think is it?" said the Lord, and continued to stand there. In the awkward silence that followed the smith's mother slowly entered to call him home for his lunch. She was old, with wrinkled face, stiff joints and a crooked back.

"You watch this," said the Lord, and led her to the forge

fire, where he restored her youth and made a lovely young maiden of her.

"Well I never," said the smith incredulously. "I'll say it again – you are not such a bad smith after all. I have learnt something this morning, but that sign over my door still calls me the 'Master over All Masters.'" Then, still shaking, he went home for his lunch, followed by a mother who looked younger than he was. After lunch he returned, and his visitors were still there. At the same time another man brought a horse to be shod.

"I will do that straight away in an instant," boasted the smith. "I have learnt a new, improved, faster way this morning."

Then he cut all the horses legs off. He didn't see why he should waste time and effort going backwards and forwards for each individual leg, and took them all to lie in the furnace together. He built up the fire, blew the bellows and not surprisingly the legs were burnt to ashes. He had to pay the owner of the horse a lot of money in compensation.

An old beggar lady was passing by, so he thought maybe he would do better at the other trick he had learnt. Kicking and screaming for her life she was dragged into the furnace.

"Do not struggle, I am going to do you the power of good," shouted the blacksmith, "and I will not even charge you." But the poor old woman went the same way as the horse's legs and was burnt to ashes.

"That was a bad thing to do," said the Lord.

"I was only trying to help her," said the blacksmith trying to excuse himself. "I doubt that she will be missed. It is a shame on the Devil though for not keeping to our bargain up over the door."

"If you could have three wishes from me, what would they be?" asked the Lord.

"If you give them to me I will soon tell you," replied the

blacksmith eagerly, so he was granted the three wishes.

"My first wish would be that anyone who climbs up that pear tree has to stay up there four years[56] or until I tell them to come down," said the Blacksmith carefully. "Then second, that anyone who I ask to sit in my chair just there has to stay there four years or until I give them permission to get up."

The blacksmith paused for thought and then continued: "Last of all, I wish that anyone who creeps into the steel purse I made, which is in my pocket, will have to stay there four years or until I say so."

Although he had been quiet up until now, St. Peter was annoyed. "You have wished the wishes of a wicked man," he rebuked. "You would have done better to have asked for God's grace and goodwill."

"Huh, I dare not ask for anything as mighty as that," replied the smith, and the Lord and St. Peter said goodbye and left him.

When the seven years were up, the Devil called upon him, as was their contract. "Are you ready?" he grinned.

"Nearly," replied the smith, "just let me finish this job, straightening this nail I am making. It will not take a moment. You must have had a long hard journey – why not help yourself to a pear from that tree to refresh yourself?" Not suspecting anything, the Devil climbed the tree, but found that he could not get down again, and that the smith just laughed at his complaints and suggested that he "just rest there a while". It was four long years before he let him come down, as he had promised to do, and the Devil was thin with hunger, thirsty through lack of drink and angry he had not been able to torment anybody for such a long time.

"You must be ready to come with me now, and finished that job," snapped the Devil.

"Oh yes, I have finished straightening the nail thank you very much, but need to sharpen the point," apologised the smith. "Sit down in that chair and rest for a minute, and I will be done."

The Devil sat down, feeling stiff from four years in the pear tree, and not seeing how a minute or two more would make much difference. Of course, he was stuck there on the chair for another four years.

The Devil complained and begged for that four years to be let up, but the smith assured him that this batch of iron was very hard to work, and after all, he was sat in an easy chair. Eventually, he promised that he would let him get up if he promised not to come for him until the minute of another four years were over. The Devil had little option but to promise, and was as good as his word. He was actually frightened of what would happen to him next, so he sped out of the door as fast as his stiff old legs would move, and did not return until another four years were up.

"You had better be ready this time," said the Devil, anxious not to sit down anywhere.

"Oh yes, I am ready as promised," said the blacksmith, "but got to wondering about your infernal powers in the last few years. Is it true what some folk say that you can make yourself very small? I did not believe them – it sounds so ridiculous."

"I certainly can," replied the Devil indignantly. "I can prove my wonderful powers right now in front of you if you like," he said confidently.

"I bet you can't make yourself small enough to get inside my purse," ventured the blacksmith. "I think I might have lost some money from it and want to know if there is a hole in the bottom."

"You will not need money where I am taking you, but of course I can!" retorted the Devil and did just that, and the purse snapped shut above his head. "It is fine" reported the Devil, "You can let me out again now."

"I'm glad it is okay, but you cannot be too careful, so I will just weld the links together for safety's sake." With that he tossed the metal purse into his burning hot furnace.

"Aggh!" cried the Devil. "Don't do this – I am still inside!"

"Oh yes, that is true," said the blacksmith smiling. "Yet it is a good old blacksmith saying that you should strike when the fire is hot." With that he took the glowing purse out of the furnace, laid it on his anvil and started to hit it as hard as he could with his very largest hammer.

"No! No!" screamed the Devil. "Stop and I will never come for you anymore."

"Alright," said the smith, "I think the links are pretty well welded now. Make your promise, and I will let you out." That was all done, and the Devil went hurriedly back to Hell, where the punishments did not seem half as bad to him now.

A few years after the blacksmith got to thinking that one day when he died he may have to face the Devil again, since from what St. Peter had said he could not be sure of getting into Heaven. He thought how he maybe should not have made such an enemy of the Devil. So he set off from the forge to find him, with his big hammer over his shoulder, since you never know when such a tool may come in handy. Along the way he met a tailor, who was going in the same direction. They walked and talked together until they met a fork in the road. A narrow path led up towards Heaven, whilst a wide path led downwards to Hell.

They parted there, as the tailor was going hopefully try to get into Heaven, but the blacksmith thought he ought to find out how things would be between himself and the Devil in Hell, since as he said, they already knew each other.

With the downward path and his much bigger stride, he moved faster than the weedy little tailor. He spoke to the watchman on the gate and told him to tell his master the Devil that an old friend the smith had come visiting, and he would remember him by his purse, chair and pear tree. When the Devil heard who it was he commanded his demons to keep him locked out and send him away, because he would destroy the place if let in.

"Lock all nine locks of the gates of Hell," he shook, "and put an extra-large padlock on to be sure!"

The smith understood that there was no home for him there, so made haste back to the fork in the road and up towards Heaven. As he got there, St. Peter was opening the gate a little bit, just enough to let the little tailor in. The blacksmith sprinted towards the gates and threw his hammer into the gap, jamming them open, and so found a place at last.

Chapter 9

British Folk Songs and Traditions

To survey all the world's folk traditions for blacksmith related songs, stories and traditional customs would demand a volume much larger than this one. I have tried to incorporate a taste of them in the preceding chapters, but wanted to reflect on a few just from the British Isles. Inevitably there will be foreign variants for some of them in existence.

Song: The Two Magicians

There is / was a belief that magicians can shapeshift into other creatures and objects. In this song (which has dozens of British variants) our blacksmith is our black magician trying to competitively overcome the female white magician, and take her virginity. There can be a large number of verses, but I will give a shorter sample to show the idea:

She looked out of the window as white as any milk
And he looked into the window as dark as any silk

(Chorus)
Hullo, Hullo Hullo you cold black smith, you'll do me no harm
You never shall my maidenhead that I have kept so long
I'd rather die a maid, But then again she said, and be buried all in
    my grave
Than I should have a nasty husky dusty fusty cold black smith – a
    maiden I will die.

Then she became a duck, a duck all on a stream
And he became a water dog and fetched her back again
(Chorus)

Then she became a hare, a hare all on the plain
And he became a greyhound dog and fetched her back again
(Chorus)

Then she became a fly, a fly all in the air
And he became a spider and fetched to his lair
(Chorus)

Then she became a nun, a nun all dressed in white
And he became a chanting priest and prayed for her by night
(Chorus)

Then she became a sheet, a sheet all on a bed
And he became an eiderdown and gained her maidenhead
(Chorus)

The Anvil

Of all the tools in a forge, the anvil is always the centre of operations, so has along with the hammer become a symbol of the blacksmith. It has been used to take oaths on and get married over. A couple of blacksmiths that I know (living opposite ends of my native East Anglia) have coins underneath their anvils. They cannot really explain why, other than to say it has always been the traditional custom to bring luck. In what can be a potentially very dangerous business it is probably as well not to tempt fate.

The anvil could be used for healing too: in Northern England there used to be a custom of taking a sickly child who was under a bad spell to a forge early in the morning.[76] Ideally the smith had to be of the 7th generation of smiths in his family. The child would be laid naked on the anvil, and the smith would raise his hammer to strike it three times. He would actually lower it gently onto their body. (Probably not advisable to try this today!) I am guessing that it would be seen as driving the curse out by being frightened of being hit.

I have already mentioned the popularity of the Horseman's Guilds in East Anglia and Scotland. They kept their horse whispering secrets well, and had a rule not to write things down, so it is not surprising that so little evidence survives. I only know of one folk song in Great Britain that furtively alludes to it. In a humorous Scots song called *Nicky Tans*, (the method of tying or strapping the bottoms of trouser legs) a single line in verse 2 refers to *"I had to get the horseman's grip and word."*[77]

There is a record of a special charm for drawing nails out of the horse's frog and healing the wound at Alcombe, Somerset.[78] It is only told to one person at a time, which in 1939 was the daughter of the late smith. I have been unable to find out if it still survives. The same source also mentions a smith in West Cornwall who was a "blood charmer" – able to successfully staunch severe bleeding of another person.

Song: A Blacksmith Courted Me

This song is much less obvious in its magical content than *Two Magicians*, yet it does bring out the virile image of a blacksmith, clearly attractive to the girl abandoned in the song, which was collected by Ralph Vaughan Williams in this form from a Mrs. Ellen Powell of Westhope, Herefordshire, in 1909.

There is a repeated phrase: *"With his hammer in his hand he looked so clever."* Whilst one has to be careful not to read too much meaning into something that may be unintended, it could possibly be read in an altogether different way than expected: the hammer in his hand can be symbolically phallic. If you doubt this consult the story of the Norse god Thor who has to get his hammer back from a giant who has stolen it. He goes in the unlikely disguise of a potential bride, because he (and the audience for the story) knows that at a crucial part of the Norse Heathen wedding ceremony it is laid in the lap of the bride.

Secondly, the use of the word "clever". We think of it today as quite an innocent word, and one we may enjoy being described as. In older meanings of the word it can mean something not quite so complimentary: if you know the phrase "too clever by half" you will understand the theme of knowing more than is good for you. Originally "clever" *could* discretely include magical knowledge.

A blacksmith courted me
Nine months and better
He fairly won my heart
Wrote me a letter.
With his hammer in his hand
He looked so clever
And if I was with my love
I would live forever.

But where is my love gone
With his cheeks like roses
And his good black Billycock on
Decked around with primroses?
I fear the shining sun
May burn and scorch his beauty
And if I was with my love
I would do my duty.

Strange news is come to town
Strange news is carried
Strange news flies up and down
That my love is married.
I wish them both much joy
Though they can't hear me
And may God reward him well
For the slighting of me.

Don't you remember when

You lay beside me
And you said you'd marry me
And not deny me?
If I said I'd marry you
It was only for to try you
So bring your witness love
And I'll not deny you.

Oh, witness have I none
Save God Almighty
And may he reward you well
For the slighting of me.
Her lips grew pale and wan
It made a poor heart tremble
To think she loved a one
And he proved deceitful.

A blacksmith courted me
Nine months and better
He fairly won my heart
Wrote me a letter.
With his hammer in his hand
He looked so clever
And if I was with my love
I would live forever.

Horseshoes

I have seen and heard a lot of arguments about which way a horseshoe should be hung to bring luck to a building. This following American description[79] reflects the most popular views I have heard, but feel free to disagree!

Some traditions say to hang them with the heel (*points*) up, to keep the luck from running out. Others say to hang them with the heel down, so that the luck will flow out of them onto those who walk underneath. Some traditions say that the shoe must be used, not new; that it must be found, not purchased; and that it's only lucky for the person who found it.

Generally, in North America, consensus is that it should be hung heel up, over or beside the door of your home. The exception to the heels-up rule is in a blacksmith's shop – where they should be hung heels down, so that the luck flows out onto all those who pass beneath. Because it is the smith, or farrier, who imparts the shoe with its luck there is no fear of the luck running out.

Chapter 10

Working with the Mythology

Inevitably, beyond the need of readers who merely want to read about a subject that they may have an interest in, or as part of research for another project, there are those who wonder "where do I go with this next?" You could of course start reading even more about the subject, in print or on the internet, but how about one of these suggestions?

Mineralogy

Do you actually now how to identify metals or the rocks that they are extracted from? There are some specialist books on the subject and some natural history museums have labelled collections to examine. You could even start your own collection, or specialise in the volcanic science named after the Roman god of smithing, volcanology.

Visiting

If you are interested in visiting places, then do visit the marvellous Wayland Smithy stone chamber on the Ridgeway, but take time to seek out local connections to blacksmith legends. For example, in my home town of Ipswich, Suffolk, there is a carving of a blacksmith on the corner post of the ancient Oak House, in Northgate Street. Some believe he is a reference to the Wayland Smithy. Near Watton, Norfolk, is Wayland Wood, connected not just to the blacksmith god but the place where legends have it that both the Babes in the Wood (from nearby Griston Hall) were abandoned, plus the head of the martyred King Edmund, guarded by a wolf. If you visit Scotland why not visit the famous Gretna Green marriage smithy and museum? There are lots of possibilities, including volcanoes, museums and a few traditional blacksmiths that are still operating, or even large industrial sites that occasionally allow visitors.

Pathworking

If physical travel is not possible, why not construct a pathworking meditation in your head, based upon your particular favourite myths. There is guidance how to do this effectively and safely in my book *Pathworking*.[80] Such creative visualisations can be simply fun, or a way of accessing greater understanding or knowledge.

Practical Projects

Another more practical way of experiencing blacksmithing is to go on a course. I have met people who have been enthralled to spend a weekend smelting metal and creating their very own personal knife or other object, to their enormous pleasure. You could alternatively try to complete a craft project in metal at home, or learn a valuable skill at college such as welding. There are always lots of books and advice on the internet how to do this. Some historic sites have visiting specialist re-enactors who can demonstrate traditional blacksmith methods. Why not volunteer to help someone like that – bellows have to be pumped for hours sometimes, so they may appreciate some assistance.

Ritual

If you intend, as a Pagan, to invoke a blacksmith god within a ritual, I would urge caution. (Why do boring people always advise "don't try this at home?" – I just recommend making sure you do it right.) Invite him cordially. He is a powerful force that a mere mortal should not try to "command". I was always taught the manners of saying please and thank you. Why should we not use those courtesies when dealing with a deity? I am sure most people would try to act politely to royalty or a president.

Make sure that the deity is appropriate to your form of ritual and the mythology or geography you are involved in. There are some old forms of witchcraft in which metal objects are specifically excluded from the circle, so I would presume it inappropriate to work with a smith god there. It would also seem illogical for someone of a Celtic persuasion to invoke an African smith god in Scandinavia. Keep to one culture at a time, as the gods of one may not like the gods of another, or understand a culture which is foreign to them.

Offer gifts that are suitable: incense carried on fire, a piece of iron or other metals, and a proper ritual fire to make them feel at home. Maybe you could even decorate an altar with hammer, tongs or bellows. Be certain of your intentions beforehand – I would not want to be invited somewhere and arrive to find that my hosts had no idea what they wanted of me or how to treat me. It would seem appropriate to treat gods the same. Maybe you want assistance with a craft project, or blessings for the construction of a bridge or aircraft. Alternatively you may just wish to honour and thank a god who has given you gifts in the past. There is no single right way to conduct a ritual, and they are much more meaningful and personalised if they have a specific resonance to your thoughts and experience. Be sure to thank beings for their presence at the end of a ritual before closing down yourself and your sacred space.

Sculpture and Jewellery

Working with metal does not have to have a practical outcome. As well as its use in jewellery or *objets d'art*, have you ever thought of going to see an exhibition of metal sculpture, such as the work of Barbara Hepworth in St. Ives, Cornwall,[81] or Henry Moore at Snape Maltings,[82] Suffolk? A lot of metal sculpture is very tactile as well as visually stimulating. Then there are exhibitions by jewellers and craftspeople of their beautiful crafts to see and often lust after like Freyja!

Collecting

Some people are born to collect: they cherish and display their collections and become experts on the particular field that they are keen on. The downside of that can be lack of space and cash. If you collect big objects, you will soon run out of space. If you collect what everyone else collects, supply and demand are likely to put the price of what you want out of the reach of the ordinary person. However, if you are interested in metal, why not start a collection of something small, decorative and relatively inexpensive? Imagine a well presented collection of old ornate metal keys, buttons or hatpins.

Chapter 11

Modern Sacred Smith Interpretations

The stories of sacred or mighty smiths continue to inspire the modern world. Inevitably, each generation takes that inspiration and regenerates it into a modern context. Blacksmiths and forges have frequently been popular subjects for paintings in many countries, although not specifically connected to the myths in the same way as some figurative sculptures. The field is vast, but let me give you a limited taste of some other forms of modern expression of the sacred smith concept that are available. I feel that it is possible to continue if you wish to make your own personal searches, interpretations of the material and ongoing links with it.

Literature

The Sacred Sword Blacksmith is a very successful Japanese graphic novel series by Isao Miura, with illustrations by Luna and a manga adaptation by Kōtarō Yamada.

There is almost a complete genre of modern American fiction (print and digital media) based upon blacksmith stories, as well as historic tales such as *The Blacksmith at Brandywine Ridge*, a well-known American Civil war tale by Charles Skinner in 1896.[83]

English children's fiction includes Wayland's tale in Kipling's *Puck of Pook's Hill*[84] and Ursula Synge wrote the popular *Weland: Smith of the Gods*.[85]

Performing Arts

The character Smithers in the long running American cartoon series *The Simpsons* has a first name of Wayland. This is believed to be a subtle reference to Wayland Smithy, although it has to be said he bears none of that figure's character.

The film *The Horse Whisperer*[86] was based upon horse magic ideas.

In the popular TV series *Robin of Sherwood*, Series 2, Episode 6, is entitled The Swords of Wayland.

The 1938 film *The Singing Blacksmith* featured Moishe Oysher, the renowned Jewish cantor in a musical about a Jewish shtetl kuvel (village blacksmith) wanting to become a mensch (a person of honour, integrity.)

Wayland Smith appears as a god in the *Last Hero*, one of the humorous series of Terry Pratchett books. Whilst that author is a comic genius in my view, one mustn't also forget the crucial role that the falling anvil has in comedy from *Monty Python* to the *Wile E. Coyote* cartoons!

Music

The *Anvil Chorus* from the Il Trovatore opera by Verdi is maybe something of a misnomer, because the Italian name for it is *Coro di zingari*, meaning *Gypsy Chorus*. However, they are striking anvils and singing about work, women and wine.

The Song of the Blacksmith is the third movement of *Second Suite in F for Military Band* by Holst.

The *Harmonious Blacksmith* is from the Suite in E Major by Handel. It is said that the allegorical tale that inspired him to write it was of Pythagoras visiting a blacksmith to investigate why some hammers sounded in harmony with each other, dependent on the ratio of their weights.

Julian Cope included a song called *Wayland's Smithy Has Wings* on his 1992 album *The Skellington Chronicles*.

Wayland the Smith is a track by Peyote.[87]

Hephaestus – Blacksmith of the Gods is a track from the new age album *Gods of Olympus* by Clifford White. There is also a band called Hephaestus who made a track called *Hammer of the Gods*.

There was a Serbian rock band named after the Polish god

Svarog, but they are long gone. Meanwhile the Finnish deity Ilmarinen gets a song in the *Kalvala Soikoon* musical, performed by the Kotka Youth Theatre.[88] *Jubal &Tubal Cain* also get a track by the band Fire and Ice[89] on the album *Fractured Man*.

See also the folk songs of Chapter 10. If one extends the search from mythology to rock songs with hammers or anvils in them, the choice is vast. Finally, there are almost too many mentions of Wayland Smith and other sacred smiths in fantasy role playing, science fiction and computer games to even start selecting one or two representatives, but I will make the honourable exception of mentioning Mr. Spock and his fellow Vulcans in the TV and film series *Star Trek*. Although presenting as logical, ordered and unemotional, this turns out to be a method their home planet culture has adapted for a race of beings who are naturally very violent. At a few ritualised ceremonies they are allowed to be unrestrained. It is not known whether the Roman blacksmith god was an inspiration for this, but I would like to think so.

Endnotes

1. Longfellow, HW. (1992) *Favourite Poems of Longfellow*. Dover Thrift: New York
2. Frazer, JG. (1922) *The Golden Bough*. Macmillan: London
3. St. Loie appears to be an alternative early spelling for St. Loye, an abbreviated form of St. Eligius who features in Chapter 8.
4. Worshipful Company of Blacksmiths http://blacksmithscompany.org/ accessed 15/12/2013.
5. Various (1921) *The Cambridge History of English and American Literature in 18 Volumes (1907–21). Volume V. The Drama to 1642, Part One*. Putnam: New York
6. Jung, C. (1990) *Analytical Psychology: Its Theory and Practice (The Tavistock Lectures)* Ark: London
7. Homer, *The Iliad*, Book 18
8. Homer, *The Iliad 18. 136 ff (trans. Lattimore)*
9. http://www.princeton.edu/~achaney/tmve/wiki100k/docs/Cabeiri.html
10. Frazer, JG. (1922) *The Golden Bough*. Macmillan: London
11. Monbiot, G. (1994) Country Life magazine.
12. Kieti, M. & Coughlin, P. (1990) *Barking, You'll be Eaten! The Wisdom of Kamba Oral Literature*. Phoenix Publishers: Nairobi
13. Simpson, WK. (2003) *An Egyptian Statuette of a Phoenician God*, Metropolitan Museum of Egyptian Art: New York. www.metmuseum.org/pubs/bulletins/1/pdf/3258013.pdf.ban nered *15/12/2013*
14. Lawrence, RM. (2003) *Magic of the Horse Shoe*. Kessinger: London
15. Tanya M. Champaco Mendiola, *Folktale: Chaife's Lost Soul*, referenced December 1, 2013, © 2009 Guampedia™, http://guampedia.com/chaife-folktale
16. Thompson, T. 1945.

17. Vigilant (1917) *The Blacksmith in Legend and History. Westralian Worker, 28 September 1917, page 5:* Australia
18. Griffiths, B. (1996) *Aspects of Anglo Saxon Magic.* Anglo Saxon Books: Hockwold-cum-Wilton
19. Rodrigues, L. (1993) *Anglo Saxon Verse Charms, Maxims & Heroic Legends.* Anglo Saxon Books: Pinner
20. Grimm, J. (1854) *Deutsches Wörterbuch.* Weidmann: Leipzig
21. Kipling, R. (1906) *Puck of Pook's Hill.* Macmillan: London
22. Scott, W. (1822) *Kenilworth.* Penguin: Harmondsworth
23. Pollington, S. (2011) *The Elder Gods.* Anglo Saxon Books: Little Downham
24. Modern English translation from www.anglo-saxons.net accessed 7/12/2013
25. Alexander, M. (1966) *The Earliest English Poems.* Penguin: Harmondsworth
26. Porter, J. (1991) *Beowulf* (verse 455) Anglo Saxon Books: Pinner
27. Alexander, M. (1966) *The Earliest English Poems.* Penguin: Harmondsworth.
28. Griffiths, B. (1996) *Aspects of Anglo Saxon Magic.* Anglo Saxon Books: Hockwold-cum-Wilton
29. Pickering (1829) *King Alfred's Anglo-Saxon Version of Boethius De Consolatione Philosophiæ.*
30. Sebillot, P. (1894) *Legendes et Curiosites des Metiers.* Flammarion: Paris
31. Larrington, C. (1996) *The Poetic Edda.* Oxford University Press: Oxford
32. Steinbeck, J. (1977) *The Acts of King Arthur and his Noble Knights (from the Winchester manuscripts of Thomas Mallory and other sources.* Book Club/ OUP: London & Oxford
33. Poem by Iorweth Fynglwyd (c. 1480-1527)
34. Koch, John T. (2005). *Celtic Culture: A Historical Encyclopedia.* ABC-CLIO: UK
35. Lady Guest, C. (2013) *The Mabinogion: from Medieval Welsh*

Manuscripts. CreateSpace: UK

36. Fee, C (2001) *Gods, Heroes & Kings.* Oxford University Press: US

37. Original source from www.Zeluna.net 15/12/2013

38. Howden, E. (1988) *The Blacksmith and the Fairies and Other Scottish Folk-Tales.* Floris Books: UK

39. The term *ceann-ileach* is translated by Rev Pattieson as "Sword-hilt of a shape peculiar to those manufactured in Islay." in Campbell J.F. (1890) *Popular Tales of the West Highlands Vol. 2.* Alexander Gardner: Paisley & London

40. http://www.polishtoledo.com/pagan accessed 10/12/2013

41. The basic story was collected by Jean-Pierre Liégeois in Macedonia, but there are many variants of it surviving around the world.

42. www.eskimo.com accessed 17/12/2013

43. http://zeluna.net/russian-fairy-tale.html accessed 13/12/2013

44. http://zeluna.net/russian-fairy-tale.html accessed 13/12/2013

45. Genesis 4:22

46. Griffiths, A. www.patheos.com accessed 22/11/2013

47. http://encyclopediaoffreemasonry.com/t/tubal-cain accessed 24/12/2013

48. Josephus, (CE 93) *Antiquities of the Jews.*

49. http://www.clanoftubalcain.org.uk accessed 12/12/2013

50. Cochrane, R. (2002) *The Robert Cochrane Letters.* Ed. M Howard Capall Bann: Milverton

51. Jackson, N. & Howard, M. (2000) *The Pillars of Tubal Cain.* Capall Bann: Chievely.

52. Pennick, N. (1989) *Practical Magic in the Northern Tradition.* Aquarius: London

53. Nash, F. (1935) The Legend of St. Dunstan & the Devil *in Dorset Shell Guide.* Shell: London

54. Smith, A. (1994) *Sixty Saxon Saints.* Anglo Saxon Books: Hockwold-cum-Wilton

55. http://www.bridgetorussian.com/files/Encyclopedia_Russia

n___Slavic_Myth_Legend.pdf 11/12/2013

56. The choice of the multiple 4 is unusual in folk stories: it is more usual to have 3, 7 or 9 as the numbers, but I have left the original figure in deliberately to show that there are exceptions.

57. Kalafut, M. (2009) *Finnish Mythology: Deities & Demons, Heroes & Humans* http://molly.kalafut.org 8/12/2013

58. Koppana, K. (2003) *Snake Fat and Knotted Threads: An Introduction to Finnish Traditional Healing Magic.* Heart of Albion: Loughborough

59. Pentikäinen, Juha Y. (1999). *Kalevala Mythology,* expanded ed. Translated by Ritva Poom. Bloomington: Indiana University Press

60. Kalafut, M. *Runo "Väinämöinen's Promise"* http://molly.kala fut.org/mythology/Finnish/pantheon.html 8/12/2013

61. Kalafut, M. *Runo 9* http://molly.kalafut.org/mythology /Finnish/pantheon.html 8/12/2013

62. Bosley, K. (1992) *The Kantelar.* Oxford University Press: Oxford

63. http://en.wikipedia.org/wiki/File:Freyja_in_silver.jpg accessed 8/12/2013

64. Known as Thunor to the Anglo Saxons

65. Wayland Smith is also credited with making him the sword Balmung in Coleman, AJ. (2007) *Dictionary of Mythology.* Arcturus: London

66. Griffiths, B. (1996) *Aspects of Anglo Saxon Magic.* Anglo Saxon Books: Hockwold-cum-Wilton

67. Crossley-Holland, K. (1980) *The Norse Myths.* Penguin: Harmondsworth

68. Keightley, T. (2008) *The Fairy Mythology: Illustrative of the Romance and Superstition of Various Countries.* Forgotten Books: London:

69. Larrington, C. (1996) *The Poetic Edda.* Oxford University Press: Oxford

70. Wagner, R. (1874) *Der Ring des Nibelungen*.
71. There is also another opera *Sigurd* on a similar theme by Ernest Reyer. JRR Tolkien wrote *The Legend of Sigurd & Gudrún*, and William Morris composed an epic poem entitled *The Story of Sigurd the Völsunga and the Fall of the Niblungs*.
72. Hatto, AT. (1969) *The Nibelungenlied*. Penguin: Harmondsworth
73. Guerber, HA. (1909) *Myths of the Norsemen*. Harrap: London
74. Bellows, H.A. (1936) *Þiðrekssaga* http://www.sacred-texts.com/neu/poe/poe17.htm accessed 14/12/2013
75. http://www.britishmuseum.org/explore/highlights/highlight_objects/pe_mla/t/the_franks_casket.aspx accessed 14/12/2013
76. Henderson (1923) *Folk-Lore of the Northern Countries of England*. BiblioLife: UK
77. http://www.kinglaoghaire.com/site/lyrics/song_304.html accessed 11/11/2013
78. Hole, C. (1940) *English Folklore*. Batsford: London
79. http://theforgery.ca/?tag=patron-saint-of-blacksmiths accessed 12/12/2013
80. Jennings, P. & Sawyer, P. (1993) *Pathworking*. Capall Bann: Chievely
81. http://www.tate.org.uk/visit/tate-st-ives/barbara-hepworth-museum-and-sculpture-garden accessed 14/11/2013
82. http://www.snapemaltings.co.uk/event/sculpture-by-henry-moore/ accessed 14/11/2013
83. http://www.sacred-texts.com/ame/lol/lol074.htm accessed 12/12/2013
84. Kipling, R. (1906) *Puck of Pook's Hill*. Macmillan: London
85. Synge, U (1972) *Weland: Smith of the Gods*. Bodley Head: UK
86. *Horse Whisperer* (1998) directed / starring Robert Redford was based on a 1995 book of the same name by Nicholas Evans.
87. http://peyote.bandcamp.com/track/wayland-the-smith accessed 12/10/2013

88. http://www.youtube.com/watch?v=HUoseZXuKFQ accessed
     13/10/2013
89. http://www.last.fm/music/Fire+%252B+Ice/_/Jubal+and
     +Tubal+Cain accessed 13/10/2013

Selected Bibliography and References

Alexander, M. (1966) *The Earliest English Poems*. Penguin: Harmondsworth

Bosley, K. (1992) *The Kantelar*. Oxford University Press: Oxford

Campbell JF. (1890) *Popular Tales of the West Highlands Vol. 2*. Alexander Gardner: Paisley & London

Cardale. (1829) *King Alfred's Anglo-Saxon Version of Boethius De Consolatione Philosophiæ* Pickering: London

Cochrane, R. (2002) *The Robert Cochrane Letters*. Ed. M Howard Capall Bann: Milverton

Coleman, AJ (2007) *Dictionary of Mythology*. Arcturus: London

Crossley-Holland, K. (1980) *The Norse Myths*. Penguin: Harmondsworth

Fee, C. (2001) *Gods, Heroes & Kings*. Oxford University Press: US

Ford, DN. (1994) *The Legend of St. Dunstan & the Devil*. G. Monbiot Country Life magazine.

Frazer, JG. (1922) *The Golden Bough*. Macmillan: London

Griffiths, B. (1996) *Aspects of Anglo Saxon Magic*. Anglo Saxon Books: Hockwold-cum-Wilton

Grimm, J. (1854) *Deutsches Wörterbuch*. Weidmann: Leipzig

Guerber, HA. (1909) *Myths of the Norsemen*. Harrap: London

Hatto, AT. (1969) *The Nibelungenlied*. Penguin: Harmondsworth

Helmbrecht, M. (2012) *A Winged Figure From Uppåkra*. Fornvännen 107. Stockholm.

Henderson. (1923) *Folk-Lore of the Northern Countries of England*. BiblioLife: UK

Hole, C. (1940) *English Folklore*. Batsford: London

Homer. (1951) *Iliad* trans. Lattimore. University of Chicago: Chicago

Howden, E. (1988) *The Blacksmith and the Fairies and Other Scottish Folk-Tales*. Floris Books: UK

Jackson, N. & Howard, M. (2000) *The Pillars of Tubal Cain*. Capall

Bann: Chievely.

Jennings, P. & Sawyer, P. (1993) *Pathworking*. Capall Bann: Chievely

Jung, C. (1990) *Analytical Psychology: Its Theory and Practice (The Tavistock Lectures)* Ark: London

Keightley, T. (2008) *The Fairy Mythology: Illustrative of the Romance and Superstition of Various Countries*. Forgotten Books: London

Kieti, M. & Coughlin, P. (1990) *Barking, You'll be Eaten! The Wisdom of Kamba Oral Literature*. Phoenix: Nairobi

Kipling, R. (1906) *Puck of Pook's Hill*. Macmillan: London

Koch, J T. (2005) *Celtic Culture: A Historical Encyclopedia*. ABC-CLIO: UK

Koppana, K. (2003) *Snake Fat and Knotted Threads: An Introduction to Finnish Traditional Healing Magic*. Heart of Albion: Loughborough

Lady Guest, C. (2013) *The Mabinogion: from Medieval Welsh Manuscripts*. CreateSpace: UK

Larrington, C. (1996) *The Poetic Edda*. Oxford University Press: Oxford

Lawrence, RM. (2003) *Magic of the Horse Shoe*. Kessinger: London

Longfellow, HW. (1992) *Favourite Poems of Longfellow*. Dover Thrift: New York

Nash, F. (1935) The Legend of St. Dunstan & the Devil in *Dorset Shell Guide* Shell: London

Pennick, N. (1989) *Practical Magic in the Northern Tradition*. Aquarius: London

Pentikäinen, JY. (1999). *Kalevala Mythology*, Trans Poom. Bloomington: Indiana University Press.

Pollington, S. (2011) *The Elder Gods*. Anglo Saxon Books: Little Downham

Porter, J. (1991) *Beowulf*. Anglo Saxon Books: Pinner

Rodrigues, L. (1993) *Anglo Saxon Verse Charms, Maxims & Heroic Legends*. Anglo Saxon Books: Pinner

Scott, W. (1822) *Kenilworth*. Penguin: Harmondsworth

Sebillot, P. (1894) *Legendes et Curiosites des Metiers*. Flammarion: Paris

Simpson, WK. (2003) *An Egyptian Statuette of a Phoenician God*. Metropolitan Museum of Egyptian Art: New York.

Smith, A. (1994) *Sixty Saxon Saints*. Anglo Saxon Books: Hockwold-cum-Wilton

Steinbeck, J. (1977) *The Acts of King Arthur and his Noble Knights (from the Winchester manuscripts of Thomas Mallory and other sources*. Book Club/ OUP: London & Oxford

Synge, U (1972) *Weland: Smith of the Gods* Bodley Head: UK

Thompson, L. (1945) *The Native Culture of the Marianas Islands*. Volume 185 of Bernice P. Bishop Museum bulletin. Honolulu: The Museum.

Torres, RT. (1991) *Selected Marianas Folklore, Legends, Literature: A Critical Commentary*. M.A. Thesis. San Diego State University, USA

Various (1921) *The Cambridge History of English and American Literature in 18 Volumes*. Putnam: New York

Vigilant. (1917) *The Blacksmith in Legend and History*. *Westralian Worker*, 28 September 1917, Australia

Moon Books invites you to begin or deepen your encounter with
Paganism, in all its rich, creative, flourishing forms.